Collins

Work on your
Grammar
Pre-intermediate A2

Collins

HarperCollins Publishers
77-85 Fulham Palace Road
Hammersmith
London W6 8JB

First edition 2013

Reprint 10 9 8 7 6 5 4 3 2 1 0

© HarperCollins Publishers 2013

ISBN 978-0-00-749955-7

Collins® is a registered trademark of HarperCollins Publishers Limited

www.collinselt.com

A catalogue record for this book is available from the British Library

Typeset in India by Aptara

Printed in Italy by LEGO SpA, Lavis, (Trento)

The material in this book has been written by a team from Language Testing 123, a UK-based consultancy that specializes in English language assessment and materials. The units are by Richard Gubbin and have been based on material from the Collins Corpus and the Collins COBUILD reference range.

www.languagetesting123.co

Contents

Introduction

Welcome to *Work on your Grammar – Pre-intermediate (A2)*.

Is this the right book for me?

This book, *Work on your Grammar – Pre-intermediate (A2)*, helps students to learn and practise English grammar at CEF level A2. This book is suitable for you to use if you are at CEF level A2, or just below.

So, what is CEF level A2? Well, there are six Common European Framework levels. They go up from A1 for beginners, A2, B1, B2, C1 and finally C2.

If the description below sounds like you, then this is probably the right book for you. If not, choose *Work on your Grammar – Elementary (A1),* below this level, or *Work on your Grammar – Intermediate (B1),* above this level.

- I can understand and use sentences about my daily life and many common topics, such as work, family, shopping, geography, and so on.
- I can talk and write in a basic way, asking questions and explaining what I need.
- I know I make mistakes, but I try to talk about the past, present and future.

What does this book contain?

This book contains 30 units to help you learn and practise important grammar for this pre-intermediate (A2) level.

Each unit explains the **grammar point** and then there is a series of **exercises** that gives you useful practice in this particular area. The exercises are there to help you really understand the grammar point and how to use it correctly. There are different types of exercise. This helps you to see different aspects of the grammar, and it means you have a range of practice to do.

The **answers** to all the exercises are at the back of the book.

Remember! boxes highlight important information about the grammar points, so it is a good idea to read them and think about them.

I'm a student: how can I use this book?

You can use this book in different ways. It depends on your needs, and the time that you have.

- If you have a teacher, he or she may give you some advice about using the book.
- If you are working alone, you may decide to study the complete book from beginning to end, starting with Unit 1 and working your way through to the end.
- You might find that it is better to choose which units you need to study first, which might not be the first units in the book. Take control of what you learn and choose the units you feel are the most important for you.

- You may also decide to use the book for reference when you are not sure about a particular grammar point.

- You can find what you want to learn about by looking at the **Contents** page.

- Please note that, if you do not understand something in one unit, you may need to study a unit earlier in the book, which will give you more information.

Study tips

1 Read the aim and introduction to the unit carefully.

2 Read the explanation. Sometimes there is a short text or dialogue; sometimes there are tables of information; sometimes there are examples with notes. These are to help you understand the most important information about this grammar point.

3 Don't read the explanation too quickly: spend time trying to understand it as well as you can. If you don't understand, read it again more slowly.

4 Do the exercises. Don't do them too quickly: think carefully about the answers. If you don't feel sure, look at the explanation again. Write your answers in pencil, or, even better, on a separate piece of paper. (This means that you can do the exercises again later.)

5 Check your answers to the exercises using the **Answer key** at the back of the book.

6 If you get every answer correct, congratulations! Don't worry if you make some mistakes. Studying your mistakes is an important part of learning.

7 Look carefully at each mistake: can you now see why the correct answer is what it is?

8 Read the explanation again to help you understand.

9 Finally, if the unit includes a **Remember!** box, then try really hard to remember what it says. It contains a special piece of information about the grammar point.

10 Always return: come back and do the unit's exercises again a few days later. This helps you to keep the information in your head for longer.

I want to improve my grammar

Good! Only using one book won't be enough to really make your grammar improve. The most important thing is you!

Of course, you need to have a paper or electronic notebook. Try these six techniques for getting the best from it.

- *Make it real:* It's probably easier to remember examples than it is to remember rules. Often, it's better to try to learn the examples of the grammar, not the explanations themselves. For example, rather than memorizing 'You can use the present simple to talk about the future', you should learn 'My holiday starts on Monday'.

- *Make it personal:* When you're learning a new structure or function, try to write some examples about yourself or people or places you know. It's easier to remember sentences about your past than someone else's! For example, 'I'm studying art this year'.

- *Look out:* Everything you read or hear in English may contain some examples of the new grammar you're learning. Try to notice these examples. Also, try to write down some of these examples, so that you can learn them.

- *Everywhere you go:* Take your notebook with you. Use spare moments, such as when you're waiting for a friend to arrive. Read through your notes. Try to repeat things from memory. A few minutes here and there adds up to a useful learning system.

- *Take it further:* Don't just learn the examples in the book. Keep making your own examples and learning those.

- *Don't stop:* It's really important to keep learning. If you don't keep practising, you won't remember for very long. Practise the new grammar today, tomorrow, the next day, a week later and a month later.

I'm a teacher: how can I use this book with my classes?

The content of this book has been very carefully selected by experts from Language Testing 123, using the Common European Framework for Reference, English Profile, the British Council Core Inventory, the Collins Corpus and material created for *Collins COBUILD English Grammar*, *Collins COBUILD Pocket English Grammar* and *Collins COBUILD English Usage*. As such, it represents a useful body of knowledge for students to acquire at this level. The language used is designed to be of effective general relevance and interest to any learner aged 14+.

The exercises use a range of types to engage with students and to usefully practise what they have learnt from the explanation pages. There are a lot of exercises in each unit so it is not necessary for students to do all the exercises at one sitting. Rather, you may wish to return in later sessions to complete the remaining exercises.

The book will be a valuable self-study resource for students studying on their own. You can also integrate it into your teaching.

The explanations and exercises are designed for self-study, but they can be easily adapted to provide useful interactive work for your students in class.

You can use the units in the book to extend, back up or consolidate language work you are doing in class. The **Contents** will help you choose which units are most appropriate.

You may also find that you recommend certain units to students who are experiencing particular difficulty with specific language areas. Alternatively, you may use various units in the book as an aid to revision.

Lesson plan

1 Read the aim and introduction to the unit carefully: is it what you want your students to focus on? Make sure the students understand it.

2 Go through the explanation with your students. You may read it aloud to them, or ask them to read it silently to themselves. With a confident class, you could ask them to read some of it aloud.

3 If there is a dialogue, you could ask students to perform it. If there is a text, you could extend it in some way that makes it particularly relevant to your students. Certainly, you should provide a pronunciation model of focus language.

4 Take time over the explanation page, and check students' understanding using concept-checking questions. The questions will vary according to content, but they may be based on checking the time in verb tenses. For example, with the sentence, 'She came on the train that got here yesterday,' you could ask, 'When did she arrive?' This might elicit the

correct answer 'yesterday' and the incorrect answer 'tomorrow', and you would know if your students understood the meaning of the past simple verb. Or you could ask, 'Where is she now?' and correct answers would include 'here' while incorrect answers would include 'on the train'.

5 Perhaps do the first exercise together with the class. Don't do it too quickly: encourage students to think carefully about the answers. If they don't feel sure, look together at the explanation again.

6 Now get students to do the other exercises. They can work alone, or perhaps in pairs, discussing the answers. This will involve useful speaking practice and also more careful consideration of the information. Tell students to write their answers in pencil, or, even better, on a separate piece of paper. (This means that they can do the exercises again later.)

7 Check their answers to the exercises using the **Answer key** at the back of the book. Discuss the questions and problems they have.

8 If the unit includes a **Remember!** box, then tell students to try really hard to remember what it says. It contains a special piece of information about the grammar point.

9 Depending on your class and the time available, there are different ways you could extend the learning. If one of the exercises is in the form of an email, you could ask your students to write a reply to it. If the exercises are using spoken language, then you can ask students to practise these as bits of conversation. They can rewrite the exercises with sentences that are about themselves and each other. Maybe pairs of students can write an exercise of their own together and these can be distributed around the class. Maybe they can write short stories or dialogues including the focus language and perform these to the class.

10 Discuss with the class what notes they should make about the language in the unit. Encourage them to make effective notes, perhaps demonstrating this on the board for them, and/or sharing different ideas from the class.

11 Always return: come back and repeat at least some of the unit's exercises again a few days later. This helps your students to keep the information in their heads for longer.

Present continuous, present simple and *will*

Talking about the future

In this unit you learn to use different tenses to talk about the future. You learn when you use the present continuous, the present simple and **will**.

> **Sophie** Hi, Tom. What **are you doing** this weekend?
>
> **Tom** **I'm visiting** my sister in London. The train **leaves** in a few minutes. **I'll text** you when I get there.
>
> **Sophie** OK. Have a great time!

When you talk about plans for the future, you often use the present continuous.

> *What **are you doing** this weekend?*
> *I'm getting the train to London this afternoon.*
> *We're going to that new restaurant tonight.*

When you talk about something in the future which happens at a definite time, you often use the present simple. You often use a time expression too.

> *The train **leaves** in a few minutes.*
> *My holiday **starts** on Monday.*
> *When **do** your exams **finish**?*

When you promise or offer to do something in the future, you use **will**.

> *I'll text you when I get there.*
> *I'll give it back to you next week.*

You can also use **will** when you are sure about something in the future.

> *She's working late tonight. **She'll be** home after 7.00.*
> *We won't be at school tomorrow. It's a holiday.*

> *Remember!*
>
> There are three forms of **will**:
>
> - **positive**
>   You can use either **will** or **'ll**. These forms do not change.
>   ***I'll / I will** see you next week.*
>   ***They'll** be here at 6 p.m.*
> - **negative**
>   You can use either **will not** or **won't**. These forms do not change.
>   ***She won't / will not** be here until this evening.*
>   ***We won't / will not** be very late.*
> - **question**
>   ***Will you** call me when you get there?*
>   ***Will we** be home by tomorrow?*

Exercise 1

Write the present continuous form of the verb in brackets to complete each sentence, as shown.

1 Next weekend we ___*are visiting*___ (visit) my sister in Brisbane.

2 I _____ (see) Rachel on Saturday.

3 Jane and I _____ (go out) tonight.

4 Martha _____ (swim) this afternoon.

5 We _____ (have) a Halloween party on Saturday.

6 I _____ (take) Sophie out for a birthday dinner tonight.

Exercise 2

Complete the sentences by writing one word in each gap, as shown.

| are | does | will | be | is | am |

1 What time _____*will*_____ you be back tonight?

2 What time _____ your train leave?

3 He won't _____ home before midnight.

4 I _____ seeing Guy and Miranda tonight.

5 What _____ you doing this summer?

6 Where exactly in Germany _____ Liz staying?

Exercise 3

Match the questions to the answers, as shown.

1 When do you leave tomorrow?   a Saturday, August 26th.

2 Which restaurant are you going to tonight?   b We're going cycling.

3 What are you doing this weekend?   c Probably not. I won't be home before midnight.

4 Will I see you later tonight?   d We fly at 3 o'clock in the afternoon.

5 Is Rebecca coming tonight?   e That French restaurant on Hills Road.

6 What day do you come back from your holiday?   f Yes, she said so.

Exercise 4

Choose the correct word, as shown.

1 What time **does / is** your bus leave?

2 I'm **see / seeing** Paolo tonight.

3 The last train **leaves / leaving** King's Cross at midnight.

4 Are you **doing / do** anything pleasant tonight?

5 I won't **being / be** back till after 11.00.

6 When **are / do** you leave tomorrow?

Exercise 5

Match the sentence halves, as shown.

1 I'm spending

2 We're travelling

3 His flight gets

4 We're having a meeting

5 Adrian won't

6 Unfortunately, I'm

a around the US this summer.

b in at 3 o'clock in the morning.

c be back until November.

d working this weekend.

e next Tuesday to discuss the matter.

f the holidays with my family.

Exercise 6

Put the correct word in each gap, as shown.

| I'll | see | won't | meeting | doing | going |

Hi there!

I hope your afternoon is going OK. Have you remembered I'm ¹_____*going*_____
out tonight? I'm ²_____ Greg in town for a drink. I ³_____ be
late – ⁴_____ probably be back by 10. Are you ⁵_____ your exercise
class as usual?

I'll ⁶_____ you later.

Love

Ben

x

Present perfect

Talking about the past and present together

have + past participle

In this unit you learn ways to talk about the past and present together using the present perfect.

Form of the present perfect

Have + past participle

The past participle of regular verbs is formed by adding **-ed** to the infinitive.

Infinitive	Past participle	Example
cook	cooked	He has cooked dinner for us.
work	worked	Have you worked hard today?
finish	finished	She hasn't finished it.

> ### Remember!
>
> You can use a short form of **have**.
>
> *I've = I have*
> *he's = he has*
> *we've = we have*
>
> *they haven't = they have not*
> *she hasn't = she has not*

● If the infinitive ends in **-e**, you add only **-d**.

Infinitive	Past participle
live	lived

● Many common verbs have irregular forms. Here are a few.

Infinitive	Past participle
be	been
have	had
go	gone
see	seen
eat	eaten

Uses of the present perfect

You can use the present perfect

- to talk about something that happened in the past but that is still important in the present:

What's the matter, Ann?

I've lost my purse.

- to describe something that started in the past and is still happening now:

    A: *Do you know this part of town?*
    B: *Yes, **I've lived** here for ten years.*

- to talk about things you have done at some time in the past:

    ***I've been** to America three times.*
    ***I've never read** any Harry Potter books.*

- with **just** to talk about the recent past:

    ***I've just finished** my exams. I'm so happy.*
    A: *Do you want some of my chocolate?*
    B: *No thanks, **I've just eaten**.*

- with **ever** to ask questions to find out things that people have done:

    A: ***Have you ever eaten** Japanese food?*
    B: *Yes, many times.*

- with **yet** and **already**:

    ***Have you done** your homework **yet**?*
    *Don't tell me what happens at the end of the film. **I haven't seen** it **yet**.*
    *We don't need any more milk. **I've already** bought some.*

Remember!

You use **already** in positive sentences, and **yet** in negative sentences and questions.

● with **for** (for a period of time) or **since** (from a point in time):

*I've lived in Paris **since** 2010.*

*He's worked there **for** three months.*

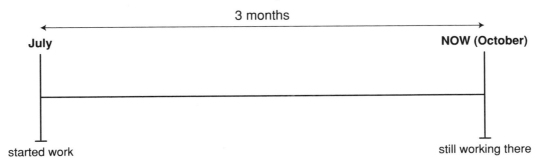

*She's been a fan **since** she saw them in concert.*

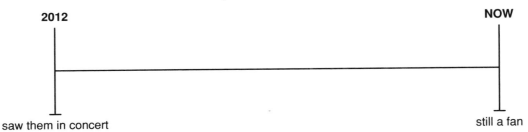

Present perfect with *been* and *gone*

Look at these examples:

*Sam's **gone** to the shops to buy a newspaper. He'll be back in a few minutes.*

This means that Sam is still at the shops.

*Julia's **been** to the shops so we've got enough food for dinner.*

This means that Julia has gone to the shops and come back.

Exercise 1

Match the sentences with the pictures, as shown.

1 He's already eaten the sandwich.

2 She hasn't drunk her coffee yet.

3 She hasn't got up yet.

4 He's already had a shower.

5 She hasn't made her bed yet.

6 She's already tidied her room.

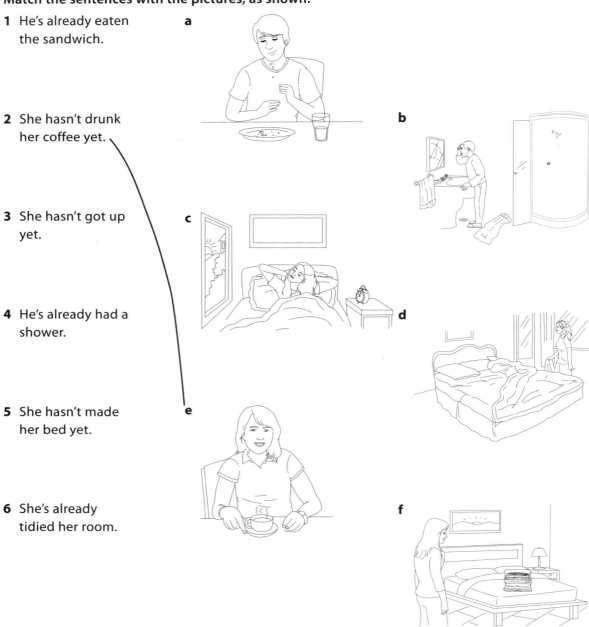

Exercise 2

Match the sentence halves.

1 Jack has worked in the same office for

2 I've lived in the same house since

3 They've been in love since

4 The food has been in the microwave for

5 Sarah has been away at university since

6 Tim's brother has been good at maths since

a he was five.

b she started last term.

c they met at school.

d three years.

e I was born.

f three minutes.

Exercise 3

Choose the correct word.

1 Have you **never / ever** eaten fish and chips?

2 I've **ever / never** been to the US.

3 Tessa has **never / ever** had a cold.

4 Has Ben **ever / never** worked in an office?

5 Have Mary and Bill **ever / never** invited you to their home?

6 Amy's teachers have **never / ever** known such a clever student.

Exercise 4

Match the sentence halves.

1 He's already put   **a** to work yet.

2 She hasn't had   **b** breakfast yet.

3 He's already cleaned   **c** the car.

4 It hasn't stopped   **d** the dishes in the cupboard.

5 She's already taken   **e** raining yet.

6 He hasn't gone   **f** the dog for a walk.

Exercise 5

Choose the correct word.

1 Sally isn't here. She's **gone / been** to the bank.

2 I'm tired because I've just **been / gone** for a swim.

3 Kevin's back now – he's just **been / gone** to the supermarket.

4 Rita's **gone / been** to buy some lunch. She'll be back in a minute.

5 Have you ever **gone / been** to the mountains?

6 Tom has **been / gone** to a meeting, so he won't be in the office today.

Exercise 6

Which sentences are correct?

1 Donald has lived in France since two years.   ❏

2 I've known my friend Sasha for a long time.   ☑

3 Liz has never learnt to swim.   ❏

4 Sarah has ever been to China.   ❏

5 Peter has washed already the dishes.   ❏

6 Claire hasn't had her lunch yet.   ❏

Prepositions
Using prepositions after certain verbs

In this unit you learn about which preposition you use after some common verbs. You also learn which common verbs have no preposition after them.

To: David

From: Alice

Subject: Last night

Hi David

How are you? I was very busy yesterday evening. I listened to music for a few minutes but my mum shouted at me because it was too loud. Then I talked to some friends on the phone. We talked about music and films.

Then I wrote an email to my friend in Australia. She's just got engaged to her boyfriend and she's marrying him next year.

After that I watched a funny DVD and laughed at all the jokes. I borrowed it from the library. I can lend it to you if you like.

Speak to you soon.
Alice

Read the email. The table below shows you which prepositions are used with which verbs, or if prepositions are needed at all.

Verb	Preposition(s)
agree	with / to
arrive	at / in
laugh	at
listen	to
look	at
shout	at
hear	–
smile	at
ask	–
talk	to, about

Verb	Preposition(s)
speak	to / about
tell	–
think	about
watch	–
write	about, to
borrow	–
lend	to
get / be engaged	to
get / be married	to
marry	–

discuss and **agree**

*I discussed the holiday **with** my parents.*
*He agreed **with** everything I said.*

speak and **tell**

*I spoke **to** him **about** the job.*
*I told him **about** my plans.*

Exercise 1

Match the sentences with the pictures.

1 He's looking at the cat.   **a**

2 She's listening to music.   **b**

3 It's thinking about food.   **c**

4 They're laughing at the TV
programme.   **d**

5 They're getting married.   **e**

6 They're arriving at school.   **f**

Exercise 2

Match the sentence halves.

1 They wrote notes   **a** from friends.

2 We all agree   **b** 'Come here!' to the cat.

3 Fred borrowed some money   **c** with you.

4 We were discussing   **d** our plans for next year.

5 Rachel is looking   **e** at the holiday photos.

6 The man shouted   **f** to their friends.

Exercise 3

Choose the correct word.

1 I lent some money **to / from** my friend.

2 You need to talk **about / to** Ellie and ask her to help you.

3 That girl is smiling **of / at** me!

4 Steve agreed **to / with** Carlos about their trip.

5 I'm going to write **about / to** my friend Teresa and tell her the news.

6 We all laughed **at / to** the funny film.

Exercise 4

Put the correct word in each gap.

| tell | think | agree | watch | ask | talk |

Hi Natasha!

Thanks for your email. I ¹_____ with you about the date of our team meeting – the 22nd will be much better than the 16th as we're all so busy at the moment. I'm going to ²_____ Heinrich Schmidt if he can come to the meeting. He can ³_____ us all about the recent business trips he's been on. We can also ⁴_____ the film that he made. Is there anything else you ⁵_____ we need to ⁶_____ about together at the meeting?

Alex

Exercise 5

Put the correct word in each gap.

| with | about | of | at | from | to |

When I was on holiday, I spent a lot of time walking the streets of the old city and taking photos
1_____ the buildings there. I also listened 2_____ local people talking
3_____ the history of their city, and I agreed 4_____ them that it is very
beautiful. I went into several museums to look 5_____ the amazing paintings in
them, and I borrowed some useful books 6_____ the big library there, too. It was a
very interesting holiday, and I'm going back again next year.

Exercise 6

Which sentences are correct?

1 Tony is going to get engaged with his girlfriend next month. ❑

2 I had to borrow some money to the bank. ❑

3 I need to discuss a few things with my colleague. ❑

4 Everyone is looking to something strange in the sky. ❑

5 The speaker is talking about the history of the city. ❑

6 We've just arrived at the train station. ❑

4

A little and *a few*

Using *(a) little* and *(a) few* when talking about things

In this unit you learn about words used to talk about quantity.

Maggie	We're cooking tonight. Let's see how much food we've got.
Daniel	OK. We've got **plenty of** rice and **lots of** tomatoes. We've also got **several** onions.
Maggie	Great! How about cheese?
Daniel	Well, we've only got **a little** and there are only **only a couple of** eggs. I think we need three or four. And there are **hardly any** mushrooms.
Maggie	OK so we need to buy eggs, cheese and **a few** mushrooms.

The table below shows you which phrases are used to show **a lot** or **not much/many**.

A lot	Not much/many
a lot of	a little
plenty of	very little
lots of	only a couple of
several	hardly any
	a few

- You use **a little / little** before uncountable nouns and **a few / few** before countable nouns:

   *There's only **a little** food in the fridge.*
   *I bought **a few** books yesterday.*

- These sentences show the difference between **few**, **a few**, **little** and **a little**:

   *I have **few** friends. = I don't have many friends.*
   *I have **a few** DVDs. = I have some DVDs.*
   *There was **very little** food left at the end of the party. = There wasn't much food left.*
   *There was **a little** food left at the end of the party. = There was some food left.*

- You can only use **several** and **a couple of** before countable nouns:

   *There are **a couple of** people waiting for you.*
   *I've been to **several** football matches this year.*

● You can use these phrases as short answers to questions. You do not use **of** in short answers:

A: How much homework have you got?
B: **Hardly any!**

A: Have you got any money?
B: **A little***.*

A: Have you seen any of his films?
B: **A couple***.*

Remember!

A lot of, lots of, plenty of and **hardly any** can be used with countable and uncountable nouns.

We've got **lots of** *milk/bananas.*
She eats **hardly any** *fruit/vegetables.*

Exercise 1

Put the correct word or phrase in each gap.

| lot | little | plenty | hardly | a few | couple |

Hi Nick

Nice to get your message. I'm afraid Anna's party didn't go so well. She invited
¹_____ of people but only ²_____ came. A ³_____ of
neighbours joined us (Paul and Sophie – I think you know them?) but ⁴_____
any of the people Anna invited from work came. I think she was quite upset. There was a
⁵_____ of food left at the end of the evening. Very ⁶_____ was eaten. It
was a shame.

Perhaps you could call Anna and have a chat?

Love
Alessandra

Exercise 2

Are the bold words correct or incorrect in the sentences, as shown?

1 There's only **a few** ☒ pasta left.
2 We're only here for **a few** ☑ days.
3 Are there any cafés near here? Yes, **a little** ☐.
4 She has **lot of** ☐ friends.
5 How many people were there? **Several** ☐ – just one or two.
6 How much milk is there? **Plenty.** ☐

Exercise 3

Complete the sentences by writing one word in each gap.

| much | several | plenty | a little | hardly | couple |

1 You're too late for the cake – I'm afraid there isn't _____ left.

2 I've got _____ of books for my holiday now.

3 I know a _____ of the teachers at Charlotte's school.

4 Jude Law is in _____ films that I hate.

5 There's _____ any coffee in the cupboard.

6 There's not much pizza left and only _____ salad.

Exercise 4

Match the sentence halves.

1 I have a couple of   a few friends.

2 The poor guy had very   b of tickets left for the show.

3 I have hardly   c of cake left, if you want it.

4 There are plenty   d cheese in the fridge.

5 There isn't much   e any money left.

6 There's a bit   f really good friends in Paris.

Exercise 5

Choose the correct word, as shown.

1 A: There were plenty of people there, weren't there? B: Yes, **a couple / lots**

2 A: There wasn't much snow last year, was there? B: No, very **little / few**.

3 A: There aren't many trees here, are there? B: No, very **little / few**.

4 A: Did Diana get many presents for her birthday? B: Yes, **a few / few**.

5 A: Is there any coffee left? B: Only **a little / a few**, I'm afraid.

6 A: How many different kinds of cake can you make? B: **Several / A little**.

Exercise 6

Decide if the pairs of sentences have the same meaning, as shown.

1 A There is little food.   ✔
  B There is not much food.

2 A There is plenty of food.   ☐
  B There is some food but not a lot.

3 A Dave has a few sweets in his pocket.   ☐
  B There are no sweets in Dave's pocket.

4 A She has few friends.   ☐
  B She hasn't got many friends.

5 A I have a few ideas for my essay.   ☐
  B I have some ideas for my essay.

6 A We had little hope that we could win.   ☐
  B We knew that we could win.

5

Possessive pronouns
Using pronouns to show who things belong to

mine, yours, his, hers, ours, theirs; one/ones; no/none

In this unit you learn to use pronouns to talk about who things belong to. You also learn about using **one, ones, no** and **none**.

You use possessive pronouns (**mine, yours, his, hers, ours, theirs**) when you talk about who things belong to.

*It's not my DVD. It's **his**.*
*See that car over there. It's **ours**.*
*Give me back that book. It's **mine**!*

You can also use **of** before a possessive pronoun.

*I know Fiona very well. She's a very good friend **of mine**.*
*Is it true that our new teacher is a neighbour **of yours**?*

Subject pronoun	Possessive pronoun
I	mine
you	yours
he	his
she	hers
we	ours
they	theirs

You use **one** and **ones** as pronouns for things.

A: I've got a few DVDs here. What do you want to watch?
*B: Well, this **one** is really funny. Let's watch that.*

*A: These trainers all look the same. Which **ones** are yours?*
*B: The **ones** with the green stripes.*

You can use **no** before a singular or a plural noun.

*There were **no** people at the tennis courts yesterday.*
*There was **no** food left at the end of the party.*

None (of) is always followed by a plural verb.

***None of** my friends are going to the concert next week.*
*I need to go shopping. **None of** my clothes fit me.*

Exercise 1

Match the sentence halves.

1 Rebecca is a cousin of mine. She's
2 Ryan was a pupil of my husband's. He was in
3 Marie was a colleague of Daniel's. They worked
4 Jane is a neighbour of Peter's. She has
5 Louise is a classmate of Ella's. They sit
6 Karen is an old friend of mine. We've known

a next to each other in Maths and English.
b together at the hospital.
c each other for years.
d the oldest daughter of my mother's sister.
e a flat in the same building.
f his class at Park School.

Exercise 2

Complete the sentences by writing one word in each gap.

ours | mine | theirs | yours | hers | his

1 I didn't have my mobile with me, so Hans lent me _____.
2 You look cold. If you haven't got a jacket, use _____ – I'm not cold.
3 We don't need to buy a tent. Angie and Julian aren't using _____, so they said we can borrow it.
4 We have the same pens, don't we? Is this mine or _____?
5 I thought this book was mine but my sister said it was _____. She's right – it's got her name in it!
6 We bought that ball last summer, don't you remember? It's definitely _____.

Exercise 3

Match the two parts.

1 It's Tom's book.
2 It's definitely Maria's mobile.
3 Those tennis rackets belong to us.
4 That umbrella belongs to me.
5 The plates are the neighbours'.
6 You brought those cups with you, Melissa.

a It's hers.
b They're yours.
c It's his.
d They're ours.
e They're theirs.
f It's mine.

Exercise 4

Complete the sentences by writing one word in each gap.

his | ours | hers | theirs | yours | mine

1 Mrs Andrews was a favourite teacher of _____, but I was the only student who liked her!
2 I met Greg at your house – I think it was at a party of _____.
3 I saw those two guys with Maria in a café yesterday. They're new friends of _____.
4 Jim and I have known Sophie and Rick for years. They're really good friends of _____.
5 I'm not sure how Adam knows George. Perhaps he's a neighbour of _____.
6 Beth goes to a different school from me. She goes to school with Isabelle and Mia. She's a classmate of _____.

Exercise 5

Put the correct word in each gap.

one | yours | ones | his | ours | hers

After the party

Everybody brought something to eat, and now I need to decide who these things belong to. I remember my aunt bringing the blue plates so these are definitely [1]_____. James brought this green one with a cake on it, so that's [2]_____. These white [3]_____ are ours and this pink [4]_____ is Sarah's. The knives and forks are definitely not [5]_____ because the ones we have look much older than that! Ah, Helen, I have a bowl here that belongs to you. This is [6]_____, isn't it?

Exercise 6

Put each sentence into the correct order.

1 is / umbrella / mine / that / .
   That umbrella is mine.

2 pen / that / yours / is / ?

3 mine / a / he's / friend / of / .

4 a / colleague / she's / Amy's / of / .

5 he / of / yours / a / friend / is / ?

6 yours / that / is / mine / or / ?

6

Possessive 's and s'

Using *s* to show who things belong to

's/s' + people, things, places

In this unit you learn to talk about who things belong to using **'s, s'** and **of**. You also learn some more irregular forms for plural nouns.

Use of the apostrophe ('s and s')

You use **'s** and **s'** to talk about people's possessions and their relation to each other.

*Silvia is **David's** wife.*
*Anna and Mark are **Jane's** cousins.*
***My parents'** best friends live in Canada.*

Sometimes, when the meaning is clear, you can use **'s** without a noun.

*I've seen that car before. It's **Diana's**.*
*Rob is at **Tom's**. (= Tom's house)*

If a name ends in **s,** you just add the apostrophe **'** to show possession.

*I think **James'** painting is better than mine.*

> *Remember!*
>
> You use **of** + *noun*, not **'s** to talk about objects.
> *The walls **of** the house are green.*
> *There's a button at the back **of** the computer.*

You can also talk about times and places using **'s** and **s'**.

*I've just got three **days'** work in a shop.*
*Bob's lucky. He's having a **week's** holiday next month.*
***London's** shopping centres are very busy in December.*

Some irregular plural nouns

Singular	Plural
half	halves
fish	fish
foot	feet
woman	women
sheep	sheep
tooth	teeth
wife	wives

Exercise 1

Match the words with the pictures.

1 The girls' cats

a

2 The boy's book

b

3 The girl's cat

c

4 The boys' book

d

5 The girl's cats

e

6 The boy's books

f

Exercise 2

Choose the correct word.

1 I brush my **tooth / teeth** every morning and evening.

2 King Henry VIII of England had six **wives / wife**.

3 Some types of bird have blue **foot / feet**.

4 The woman gave Ben and Tina **halves / half** an apple each.

5 Some of the sheep in the field **was / were** black.

6 These fish **are / is** goldfish.

Exercise 3

Write the missing words in sentence B so that it means the same as sentence A.

1 **A** This is the car that belongs to Keith.

   B This is _____*Keith's*_____ car.

2 **A** The house where my parents live is quite old.

   B _____ house is quite old.

3 **A** People say there's gold where a rainbow ends.

   B People say there's gold at the _____ a rainbow.

4 **A** I'm going on holiday for a week.

   B I'm going to have a _____ holiday.

Exercise 4

Put each sentence into the correct order.

1 dog's / what's / name / Alex's / ?

   _____

2 put / at / stairs / I've / the bottom / your coat / the / of / .

   _____

3 Wayne / new / starting / in / is / a / time / a week's / job / .

   _____

4 the / nationalities / what / students' / are / ?

   _____

5 of / the / you / what's / the hotel / name / stayed / where / ?

   _____

6 top / the / sportsmen and women / you / at / world's / can watch / the Olympic Games / .

   _____

Exercise 5

Complete the sentences by writing one word or phrase in each gap.

| of the sofa | six months' time | my wife's | London's | the back of |
| of the swimming pool | | | | |

1 The new school will open in _____.

2 The arm _____ is broken.

3 I think you'd better speak to the manager _____.

4 _____ job takes her all over the world.

5 Something was written on _____ the photograph.

6 _____ West End is where most of the theatres are.

Exercise 6

Use the word in brackets to complete each sentence.

1 My _____ (father) family came from Spain.

2 The front wheel _____ (car) was badly damaged in the accident.

3 The _____ (students) exam results made them very happy.

4 Both my _____ (parents) families were very poor.

5 Sarah was surprised by the cost _____ (tickets).

7

Articles and other words before nouns

both/all; *a/the*; zero article

In this unit you learn about using articles (**a** and **the**) before nouns. You also learn about using **both** and **all**, **every**, **other**, **another** and **no** before nouns.

Some uses of *a* and *the*

You use **the** when

● it is clear which person or thing you are talking about:

> *The street's very empty tonight.*
> *I put **the keys** on **the fridge**.*

● there is only one of these people or things:

> *I saw **the president** on TV yesterday.*
> ***The moon** is very bright tonight.*

You use **a** when

● you have not talked about something before:

> *I saw **a good film** yesterday.*
> *I think I need **a new phone**.*

● you say what jobs people do:

> *My brother's **a famous footballer**.*
> *She's training to be **a doctor**.*

Sometimes there is no article before a noun

She's	at work, at home	I'm going to	work
	in bed		bed
	at school, college, university		school, college, university
	in hospital		hospital
	in prison		prison
	in church		church

BUT

She's at	**the** cinema
	the theatre
	the bank
	the post office
	the doctor's, etc.

*My aunt's not very well. She's **in hospital**.*
*I'll be **at school** until 6 p.m. today.*
*Anna's going **to the cinema** this evening.*

> *Remember!*
>
> *He goes **to school** at 8 a.m.*
> *He gets **home** at 6 p.m.*

Words used to express quantity (how much)

You use **both** and **all** before a plural noun. You only use **both** to describe two people or things.

*I watched two DVDs last night. They were **both** fantastic.*
*I really want to go to the party. **All** my friends will be there.*
*He spent **all** his money at the shopping centre.*

You use **every** before a singular noun.

*We go to Spain on holiday **every** year.*

You use **another** before a singular noun and **other** before a plural noun. You can use words like **some**, **any**, **many** and **lots of** before **other**.

*Would you like **another** drink?*
*Don't worry. There'll be **some other** people you know there.*
*Have you visited **any other** countries?*

> *Remember!*
>
> **no** and **any**
> ***I haven't got any** time to do my homework.* (negative verb)
> ***I've got no** time to do my homework.* (positive verb)

Exercise 1

Complete the sentences by writing one word in each gap.

1 Madrid is _____ capital of Spain.

2 It was ª _____ beautiful morning. ᵇ _____ sun was shining.

3 There's _____ very pretty cat in the garden. I've never seen it before.

4 Her brother's in ª _____ army and her sister's ᵇ _____ lawyer.

5 Is there _____ supermarket near here, do you know?

6 Could you turn off all _____ lights when you leave the room, please?

Exercise 2

Choose the correct word or words.

1 What time do you go to **the work / work**?

2 I think you should go to **dentist's / the dentist's**.

3 Mark was ill and had to go to **hospital / the hospital**.

4 You look tired. I think you should go to **bed / the bed** early.

5 We often go to **the theatre / theatre** in London.

6 I need to go to **post office / the post office**.

Exercise 3

For each question, tick the correct answer, as shown.

1 Does your little girl go to
   ☐ the school yet?
   ☑ school yet?

2 We wanted to see a new film, so we went to
   ☐ the cinema.
   ☐ cinema.

3 After school, I want to go to
   ☐ the university in the United States.
   ☐ university in the United States.

4 We have to get up early and drive to
   ☐ airport.
   ☐ the airport.

5 Last week we went to
   ☐ theatre.
   ☐ the theatre.

Exercise 4

Put each sentence into the correct order.

1 all / ate / my / my brother / food / .

_____

2 like / those / dresses / both / I'd / .

_____

3 see / my / I / weekend / parents every / .

_____

4 house every / went / boys / the / to Josh's / day / .

_____

5 all / broke / the chef / the / eggs / .

_____

6 other / home / sister / my / is / at / .

_____

Exercise 5

Complete the sentences by writing one word in each gap.

1 That coffee was so good! Could I have _____ cup, please?

2 I don't like him, but the _____ people in my class think he's OK.

3 I don't like this pen. Is there _____ one I can use?

4 This cake is delicious! May I have _____ piece, please?

5 The sun's so hot here. Let's cross to the _____ side of the road and walk under the trees.

6 This is very heavy. Please use _____ your hands to carry it.

Exercise 6

Complete the sentences by writing one word in each gap.

| any | no | another | every | some | other |

1 I don't have _____ money.

2 Could I borrow _____ money, please?

3 I don't like this cheese so much. I prefer the _____ one.

4 She gave a present to _____ child in the class.

5 There's coffee, but I'm afraid there's _____ milk.

6 This is a difficult exercise. May I have _____ five minutes, please?

8

Past continuous
Talking about two events in the past

was/were + -ing

In this unit you learn about using the past continuous to talk about the past.

What was everybody doing when the clock struck midnight?

Anna **was laughing** at something and her sister, Helen, **was sleeping** in a chair. Helen's husband **was drinking** a glass of lemonade and his brother **was dancing** with his wife. Helen's two children **were watching** a film on TV.

You use the past continuous to describe continuous actions in the past.

I/he/she	was/wasn't	sleeping dancing watching TV	all night.
you/we/they	were/weren't		
Was	I/he/she	reading working	all night?
Were	you/we/they		

You can use the past continuous with the past simple to compare two actions. You use the past continuous when you describe the longer action.

*William **was running** to catch a bus **when he fell over**.*

You can compare the two actions using **when**, **while** and **as**.

*I was swimming in the sea **when** it started raining.*
*I texted my friend **while** I was waiting for the bus.*
***As** I was leaving home, the phone rang.*

You can put the two parts of these sentences in a different order:

***When** it started raining I was swimming in the sea.*

> *Remember!*
>
> You use **when** before the past simple and **while** or **as** before the past continuous.

Exercise 1

Write the correct form of the verb in brackets to complete each sentence.

1 Gemma met her husband while they were both _____ (travel) in India.

2 Where were you going when I _____ (see) you yesterday?

3 I was living abroad when the accident _____ (happen).

4 As he was _____ (wait) for Anna, he looked around the room.

5 While I was walking to the park, I suddenly _____ (have) a great idea.

6 As Paula was _____ (get) on the train, she fell and hurt her knee.

Exercise 2

Choose the correct word or words.

1 Who **were you talking to / did you talk to** when I saw you in the café yesterday?

2 While Suzi was cleaning the house, she **was finding / found** a ring under the sofa.

3 As we were eating our meal, we **were hearing / heard** a loud noise in the next room.

4 She often **listened / was listening** to music while she was working.

5 As we were **said / saying** goodbye, she gave me a present.

6 What **did you do / were you doing** while your friends were playing tennis?

Exercise 3

Complete the sentences by writing one word in each gap.

| getting | dropped | met | having | working | visiting |

1 While I was _____ Tom, I helped him with his computer.

2 Tara learned to speak Spanish while she was _____ in Madrid.

3 As I was _____ dressed, I felt a sudden pain in my arm.

4 Greta and Martin were _____ an argument when I arrived.

5 When I _____ John, he was studying at Liverpool University.

6 As Martha was giving me the glass, she _____ it and it broke.

Exercise 4

Match the sentence halves.

1 What were they doing

2 While I was waiting for my dad,

3 As we were leaving, we noticed

4 When Robert arrived, I

5 My friend Maria called

6 What did you do while

a while I was having a shower.

b was having my dinner.

c your parents were on holiday?

d I read a magazine.

e when the lights went out?

f some men outside the house.

Exercise 5

Which sentences are correct?

1 As I was checking my email, Peter came into the office. ❑

2 Someone was stealing Maria's passport while she slept. ❑

3 I watched a movie when Ben called to tell me the news. ❑

4 While Pat was shopping, I had a cup of coffee in a café. ❑

5 As we were climbing up the hill, we were noticing several black clouds in the sky. ❑

6 I was driving to my mother's house when I saw a horse in the road. ❑

Exercise 6

Choose the correct word.

The lost handbag

As I [1]**was come / am coming / was coming** home from work yesterday, I [2]**was seeing / saw / see** something on the pavement. It was a woman's handbag. I picked it up and looked in it. I found a card with a phone number. I called the number and a woman answered. 'I [3]**was cycling / to cycle / cycled** to work when I [4]**drop / was dropping / dropped** it,' she explained, 'but I only noticed a minute ago. I was very worried!'

She said she could come straight away. It was a sunny day, so while I [5]**was waiting / was wait / wait** for her, I [6]**was sitting / am sitting / sat** on a bench and read the newspaper.

9

There and *It* sentences

Using *There* and *It* at the beginning of sentences

In this unit you learn about using **There was**, **There has been**, **There will be** and **It** at the beginning of sentences.

You use **There is** and **There are** when you are talking about the present. You can also use **There + be** with other tenses.

There was/were

> *There weren't any apples so I bought oranges instead.*

There has/have been

> *There has been a lot of sport on TV this summer.*

There will be

> *There will be lots of people at the party.*

You use **It** before **be**

● to talk about the weather:

> *It was very sunny yesterday.*

● to talk about time:

> *It will be very late when we get home.*

You can also use **it** with **take**:

> *A: How long did it take to get here?*
> *B: About three hours.*

● to express your opinions:

> *It was a really good film.*
> *It's going to be a very expensive holiday.*

● to describe a scene in the past:

> *It was a cold day in December.*
> *It was a great day for swimming.*

Exercise 1

Choose the correct word.

1 There **was / wasn't / hadn't** anyone in the room when I arrived.

2 It **will / has / is** take three hours to reach Prague.

3 **Have / Was / Did** there been any phone calls for me?

4 How many people **was / were / been** there at the party?

5 **Was / Has / Did** it rain when you were in Spain?

Exercise 2

Put each sentence into the correct order.

1 building / is / in / there / a doctor / this / ?

_____

2 holiday / it / a / been / wonderful / has / .

_____

3 the house / easy / won't / to find / it / be / .

_____

4 problems / weren't / the car / there / with / any / .

_____

5 cold / night / outdoors / was / last / it / ?

_____

6 a / is / to be / storm / going / there / .

_____

Exercise 3

Choose the correct word or words.

Hi Cristina

How are you? [1]**There's / It's** strange to be so far away from you and my other friends, but some of the people at my new school are very nice. [2]**There was / It was** a bit difficult at first, but now I feel OK.

The school is good. [3]**There's been / It's been** a school here since 1820. Isn't that amazing? Anyway, [4]**there have been / it has been** a lot of changes since then!

The sports centre is very good. [5]**There was / It was** an international match here last year and I hope they'll have one again this year so I can play in it. [6]**There isn't / It isn't** easy to get into the team, but I think I can.

Write and tell me the news from home soon.

Love

Pia

Exercise 4

Decide if the pairs of sentences have the same meaning.

1 **A** It was a very crowded club.
  B The club was very crowded. ❑

2 **A** There wasn't anywhere for us to sit.
  B It wasn't easy to find our seats. ❑

3 **A** It was very late when we got home.
  B We arrived home very late. ❑

4 **A** There's going to be a big party at the end of term.
  B We're planning a big end-of-term party. ❑

5 **A** It was snowing when I left home this morning.
  B The snow started when I was walking to work this morning. ❑

Exercise 5

Which sentences are correct?

1 There were a lot of people at the concert last weekend. ❑

2 It was problem for me to understand all the rules. ❑

3 It was surprisingly easy to get into the palace. ❑

4 Has it been an accident on the motorway? ❑

5 There will be expensive to fly, so let's drive. ❑

6 There was a lovely, sunny day and the beach was crowded. ❑

Exercise 6

Write the correct form of the words in brackets to complete each sentence.

1 You're very wet! _____ (it rain)?

2 I'm still hungry. _____ (there be) any more sandwiches in that box?

3 I'm not sure if these shoes are the right colour. _____ (it be) possible to change them if I bring them back next week?

4 _____ (there be) no one at the house, so we couldn't go in and look round.

5 Why didn't you call me? _____ (there not be) a phone in the bus station?

6 I've just checked the weather forecast and _____ (it be) fine all weekend. Let's go camping.

10

Questions

Asking questions in the past and present

In this unit you learn how to ask questions in the present and the past. You learn about indirect questions and more about question words.

Direct questions in the present and past

> **How well do you know your best friend?**
>
> ① How long have you known him/her?
> ② How often do you text him/her?
> ③ When did he/she last come to your house?
> ④ Which does he/she like better, coffee or tea?
> ⑤ What was he/she doing yesterday evening?
> ⑥ How tall is he/she?
> ⑦ Why do you like him/her?

Read the quiz and look at the answers. Decide which is the best answer for each question.
A About three times a day.   B 1.6 m   C Working in a restaurant.   D Because he's very funny.
E Since we started school together.   F On Saturday morning.   G Coffee.

Answers: 1E 2A 3F 4G 5C 6B 7D

Indirect questions

You can also ask indirect questions. These can sound more polite.

> *Do you know* where the post office is? (=*Where is the post office?*)
> *Did you understand* what he was saying? (=*What was he saying?*)
> *Can you tell me* when the bank opens? (=*When does the bank open?*)

How, which, whose

You use **how** to ask for instructions to do something.

> *How do you turn the computer on?*
> *Can you tell me* **how** *I can get a passport?*

You use **which** when you are asking about a small number of things.

> *Which dress do you prefer?*
> *Which programme do you want to watch?*

To find out who something belongs to, you use **whose**.

A: **Whose** car is that outside?
B: It's mine.

Do you know **whose** those gloves are?

To find out what someone thinks about a person or thing you can use **what ... like**.

A: **What's** their new CD **like**?
B: It's great.

A: **What's** your new teacher **like**?
B: She's quite nice but she's a bit strict.

> *Remember!*
>
> Look carefully at the different verb forms in direct and indirect questions.
> *When **does** the supermarket **open**?*
> *Do you know when the supermarket **opens**?*

Exercise 1

Choose the correct words.

1 Whose glasses **these are / are these**?

2 Could you tell me when **the next train leaves / the next train does leave**?

3 Do you know why **is the door locked / the door is locked**?

4 How **you open / do you open** this cupboard?

5 How tall **your sister is / is your sister**?

6 What **is her new boyfriend / her new boyfriend is** like?

Exercise 2

Find the wrong or extra word in each sentence.

1 Which are books do you need to take with you?

2 How often times do you go to the gym?

3 Can you tell me when is the show starts?

4 He asked me where do I work.

5 How long time is the movie?

6 Why was the letter it written in French?

Exercise 3

Complete the sentences by writing one word in each gap.

1 _____ is the food like at the new restaurant?

2 _____ of these bags do you like best?

3 _____ often should I take the medicine?

4 How _____ have you been waiting here?

5 _____ much rice would you like?

6 Do you know _____ Patrick looks so angry?

Exercise 4

Match the sentence halves.

1 Does he understand
2 Could you tell me where I
3 How often are
4 How long is it
5 Do you know why
6 How long has your family

a until your holiday?
b what he needs to do?
c Jake needed so much money?
d can buy a ticket?
e the rooms cleaned?
f lived in this country?

Exercise 5

Complete the sentences by writing one word in each gap.

| which | who | like | why | long | whose |

1 How _____ did he spend in hospital?
2 Do you know _____ laptop this is?
3 _____ gave Tara the job?
4 Can you tell me _____ the trains are so late?
5 What was your hotel _____?
6 _____ dress have you decided to wear?

Exercise 6

Put each sentence into the correct order.

1 when / the / cooked / food / was / ?

_____

2 how / wall / is / the / high / ?

_____

3 are / these computers / often / checked / how / ?

_____

4 pictures / like / you / which / best / do / ?

_____

5 me how / use this machine / you / can / tell / to / ?

_____

6 was / story / to the class / whose / read / ?

_____

Adjectives

Talking about people and things, and comparatives and superlatives

be + adjective + preposition

In this unit you learn to use adjectives to talk about people and things. You also learn more about comparative and superlative forms.

When you want to describe people or things, you can use the verb **be** and an adjective.

I'm cold.
She's kind.

You can use adverbs like **very** and **really** in front of many adjectives.

Paul's very tall.
These questions are really important.

Adjectives have comparative (**taller**) and superlative (**the tallest**) forms, so you can compare two things or people.

John's house is older than mine.
She's the tallest girl in the school.

For most longer adjectives, you say **more** or **the most** before the adjective.

I think geography is more interesting than chemistry.
Clara is the most beautiful girl I know.

You can make comparisons using **not as … as …**, **less … than …** and **the least** … .

● **not as … as …**

   Simon isn't as intelligent as Anna. (Anna is more intelligent than Simon.)

● **less … than …**

   You can also use **less … than …** with most longer adjectives.

   Reading books is less interesting than playing computer games.
   (Playing computer games is more interesting than reading books.)

● **the least …**

   Why don't you buy these shoes? They're the least expensive. (the cheapest)

Some adjectives are different from the examples above.

Adjective	Comparative	Superlative
good	better	best
bad	worse	worst

You need to use a preposition after some common adjectives.

Preposition	Adjective
at	good at, the worst at
of	fond of, afraid of
with	angry with, friendly with
about	worried about, excited about
to	kind to, unkind to

*I was always **good at** maths at school.*
*My mum's really **afraid of** spiders.*
*I was late for school and my teacher was very **angry with** me.*
*I'm really **excited about** my holidays.*
*Sam was very **kind to** me on my first day at work.*
*My brother's **better** at tennis than me.*

Exercise 1

Choose the correct word or words.

1 The **tall / taller / tallest** building I saw in Paris was the Eiffel Tower.

2 Anita is **smart / smarter / smartest** than all the girls in my class.

3 It's **hot / hotter / hottest** today than yesterday.

4 This ring was the **expensive / more expensive / most expensive** in the shop.

5 This book is less **heavy / heavier / heaviest** than that one.

Exercise 2

Put the correct word in each gap.

colder	expensive	fastest	better	difficult	hardest	smaller

What I did last year

Last year was the ¹_____ year of my life. I moved to England and had to find a new

job. England is ²_____ than Greece and it rains a lot too. I had to buy a jacket and

some new boots. I live in a flat in the centre of town. It is ³_____ than my house in

Greece but more comfortable. I work in a restaurant in the town centre. The food is the most

⁴_____ in town but it is also really delicious. The job is more ⁵_____

than I thought but I am getting ⁶_____ at it.

Exercise 3

Match the two parts.

1 Mary doesn't like dogs.
2 Thomas is angry with me.
3 I am really fond of reading.
4 Jessica hates sport.
5 My brother loves animals.
6 Charles plays for a local football team.

a He is very kind to them.
b She is afraid of them.
c I forgot his birthday.
d She's really bad at it.
e I buy a new book every weekend.
f He is really good at it.

Exercise 4

Find one word that does not belong in each group, as shown.

1 **Adjectives followed by** *at*	good	busy	bad
2 **Adjectives followed by** *of*	fond	afraid	keen
3 **Adjectives followed by** *to*	kind	unkind	careful
4 **Adjectives followed by** *with*	friendly	frightened	angry
5 **Adjectives followed by** *about*	worried	excited	delicious

Exercise 5

Which sentences are correct?

1 Jackie is good at basketball because she is the tallest in her class. ☐
2 Nurses have to work hard and be kind to everyone. ☐
3 My best friend is really angry of me because I lost her most expensive ring. ☐
4 That is the less interesting film I have ever seen. ☐
5 My sister Margaret is very keen of sport. ☐
6 Who do you think has the most important job, doctors, police officers or teachers? ☐

Exercise 6

Put each sentence into the correct order.

1 the / is / best / to visit / time / you / what / ?

_____

2 about / my / I'm / new / excited / car / .

_____

3 everyone / is / in / Nick / his class / younger / than / .

_____

4 this chair / the / least / is / comfortable / .

_____

5 Jo / milk / is / chocolate / very fond / of / .

_____

6 peaches / sweetest / are / fruit / the / .

_____

12

Link words

both … and, either … or, neither … nor, not only … but also, so … that

In this unit you learn how to connect parts of sentences together.

Both … and, neither … nor

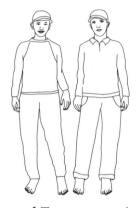

Both Dan and Tony are wearing caps.
Neither Tony nor Dan have got shoes on.

You can also use these phrases with adjectives to describe people or things.

She was both intelligent and pretty.
The book was neither original nor interesting.

You use **either … or** when there is a choice.

You can either have ice cream or fruit for dessert.
You can either buy it in a bookshop or online.

You use **not only … but also** to describe two important things about a person or thing.

The chicken was not only cold but it also tasted strange.
He's not only a famous singer but he's also made five films.

You can also use **so + *adjective*** or ***adverb* + that** as a way of describing people or things.

*The exam was **so easy** that I finished it in less than an hour.*
*She ran **so** quickly **that** I couldn't catch her.*

You can also use this phrase without **that**.

*The train was **so** slow, I was late for school.*

Exercise 1

Choose the correct word.

1 Every girl will get either a scarf **or / and** a box of chocolates.

2 Neither their family **and / nor** their friends knew they were married.

3 The club was not only small **but / or** also very dark.

4 They ran **such / so** fast that they fell over.

5 I decided to buy **both / neither** the red dress and the green one.

6 I was so angry with Adriana **nor / that** I couldn't speak.

Exercise 2

Put the correct word in each gap.

| nor | and | not only | or | so | both |

Vijay

Vijay is a great guy and ¹_____ his friends and his colleagues think he is fantastic.
At work, he is ²_____ quick, but also very careful. In fact, he is ³_____
popular that when he got married, his colleagues wanted to buy him a really nice present.

Neither his best friend ⁴_____ his parents could suggest anything, so they
decided to give him and his wife some money. Vijay said they would use it to buy either a sofa
⁵_____ some plants for their garden. He invited a lot of people to the wedding, and
both his family ⁶_____ his friends had a great time.

Exercise 3

Which sentences are correct?

1 They stole not only my passport but also my money. ❏

2 The bag was so heavy that I could carry it. ❏

3 I would like to study either medicine and law. ❏

4 I was both upset and angry when I heard the news. ❏

5 Travel around my city is neither quick or easy. ❏

6 I think I will have either the fish or the pasta. ❏

Exercise 4

Complete the sentences by writing one word in each gap.

1 You may take either an apple _____ a banana, but not both.

2 Both her parents _____ her teachers are worried about her.

3 Unfortunately, the hotel was _____ comfortable nor clean.

4 The wall was _____ high that we couldn't climb over it.

5 The path was not only steep _____ also dangerous.

6 Neither her friends _____ her family phoned her.

Exercise 5

Put each sentence into the correct order.

1 neither clever / nor funny / his behaviour / was / .

_____

2 but / also delicious / the food was / only healthy / not / .

_____

3 I was / I had / to go / to bed / so tired / .

_____

4 the bike / both the car / and / were / stolen / .

_____

5 either / scissors / or some / I need / a knife / .

_____

6 to go home / we decided / was / the weather / so bad / .

_____

Exercise 6

Match the sentence halves.

1 The tourist guide was neither interesting	a nor helpful.
2 My parents gave me both a watch	b but also my camera.
3 My shoes were so uncomfortable	c nor the email.
4 I lost not only my money	d I couldn't walk.
5 I usually travel either by bus	e and a phone.
6 We understood neither the letter	f or by train.

13

Time clauses
Using adverbs to talk about time and other connections

In this unit you learn how to use phrases with **when**, **while**, **before** and **after** to talk about when things happen. You also learn about when to use phrases with **if**, **although** and **to**.

When, while, before, after

> To: Anna
> From: Sally
> Subject: Holiday
>
> Hi Anna
> I'm getting on the plane now! I fed the cats before I left for the airport.
> Can you feed them while I'm away? I'll text you again after the plane has
> landed. See you when I get back.
> Sally

Put the events in the right order:
1 Sally gets on the plane.
2 Sally feeds the cats.
3 She leaves for the airport.
4 Sally sees Anna.
5 Anna feeds the cats.
6 Sally gets back.
7 Sally texts Anna again.
8 The plane lands.

Answers: 2, 3, 1, 8, 7, 5, 6, 4

You use **before** and **after** with a verb to show when things happen.

*He did his homework **before** he had dinner.*
*He did his homework **after** he had dinner.*

You use **when** to show that one thing happens right after another.

*She opened her presents **when** she woke up.*
*He turned on his computer **when** he got home.*

You use **while** to show that one thing happens at the same time as another thing.

*He usually does his homework **while** he watches TV.*
*She borrowed my car **while** I was on holiday.*

You can also begin the sentence with **when**, **while**, **before**, **after**.

***When** he got home, he turned on his computer.*
***While** I was on holiday, she borrowed my car.*

Exercise 6

Are the bold words correct or incorrect in this text?

Our swimming pool

At our swimming pool, there are lots of rules. For example, you ¹**mustn't** ❑ run around the pool. If you have long hair, you ²**must** ❑ wear a swimming hat, but if your hair is short you ³**aren't** ❑ have to.

Children have to be with a parent if they are ⁴**not able** ❑ to swim very well. When the pool is busy, you ⁵**haven't** ❑ dive in, and you ⁶**can** ❑ only swim for an hour.

18

Modal verbs (2)

Talking about what you might do, but aren't sure about

could, might, may, will probably

In this unit you learn about using modal verbs to talk about possibility and probability using **could**, **might**, **may** and **will probably**.

May and *might*

You use **may** and **might** to talk about something which is possible, but we are not sure about.

In the present

> **A** Have you seen David ?
> **B** He **might** be in his room.
> **A** No, he isn't. I've looked.
> **B** He **may** be at the shops then.

In the future

> **A** Have you got any plans for this evening?
> **B** I **might** go to the cinema. Do you want to come?
> **A** No thanks. I **may** just stay at home and watch a DVD.

The meaning of **may** and **might** in these sentences is the same.

> *Remember!*
>
> For negatives, you add **not** or *n't* to **might**.
> It **mightn't** rain.
> For **may**, you only add **not**.
> He **may not** come.

Could

You can also use **could** to talk about something you are not sure about in the present or future.

*Be quiet. He **could** be asleep.*
*It **could** be too hot to go to the beach tomorrow.*
***Could** we save enough money to go on holiday?*

Will probably

You use **will probably** when you are more sure about something.

*I've missed the last bus. I **could** get a taxi but **I'll probably** walk home.*

Exercise 1

Match the two parts.

1 My parents probably won't pay
2 My friends may want
3 This hot weather could
4 Your grandfather might enjoy
5 The new park will probably
6 Emma might not

a be ready yet.
b last all week.
c this music.
d to meet us this evening.
e be open in the spring.
f for my holiday.

Exercise 2

Put the correct words in each gap.

will probably be | might help | could call | might not be | may come | could walk

Getting home

Lucy: Oh no! We've missed our train.

Giles: The next one [1]_____ soon.

Lucy: No, not till the morning.

Giles: Do you think we [2]_____? It's not that far.

Lucy: Or my brother [3]_____. I [4]_____ and ask him to come with his car.

Giles: He [5]_____ in bed by now.

Lucy: He [6]_____. He often stays up very late.

Giles: OK, let's try phoning him.

Exercise 3

Choose the correct word or words.

1 I think it might **raining / rain** later.

2 Do you think you could **run / to run** ten miles?

3 My brother might not **want / wants** to go to the football match.

4 Laura probably won't **be able / to be able** to do all that work before Friday.

5 The parcel may **arrives / arrive** tomorrow.

6 I couldn't **going / go** to John's party.

Exercise 4

Which sentences are correct?

1 I'm sorry, but I might not able to come to your party. ❑

2 Be careful: that dog could easily jump over the wall. ❑

3 There may not be enough time to talk to everyone. ❑

4 Adam won't probably want a big meal. ❑

5 I have to stay at work late, so I may not joining you later at the café. ❑

6 We couldn't get home because there were no trains. ❑

Exercise 5

Put each sentence into the correct order.

1 probably / the competition / won't / our team / win / .

_____

2 to buy / could / a new computer / afford / you / ?

_____

3 a laptop / give / might / my parents / me / .

_____

4 may / for swimming / the water / be / too cold / .

_____

5 to come / I'll probably / with me / my mum / ask / .

_____

6 that Alfie / I'm sure / see / couldn't / us / .

_____

Exercise 6

Are the bold words correct or incorrect in the sentences?

1 Our teacher will probably **to give** ❑ us lots of homework.

2 Could you **asked** ❑ your dad for some money?

3 I might **stay** ❑ in Paris for another day or two.

4 Harry may **don't** ❑ arrive in time for the concert.

5 There **might** ❑ not be any tickets left now.

6 The keys could still **being** ❑ in Katie's bag.

19

Modal verbs (3)

Giving advice

should, ought to, had better

In this unit you learn about ways of giving advice using **should**, **ought to**, **had better**.

What **should** I do to win next time?

Well, you **should** train every day for two hours and you **shouldn't** go to bed so late or eat so many hamburgers. You also **ought to** buy some better running shoes. The next race is in two days so you**'d better** start training immediately.

Training programme	
eat hamburgers	✗
buy new shoes	✓
start training now	✓
go to bed late	✗
train for two hours a day	✓

Should, ought to

You use **should** and **ought to** when you give advice or ask for advice.

*You **should** eat more vegetables.*
*You **shouldn't** work so hard. You **ought to** relax a bit more.*
*I've lost my passport. What **should** I do?*

Had ('d) better

You can also use **had better** for giving advice.

*You**'d better** get more petrol. It's very low.*

> ## Remember!
>
> In negative sentences you say **had ('d) better not**.
> *We're having a big meal later so you**'d better not** eat too much now.*

Exercise 1

Which sentences are correct?

1 You shouldn't to be rude to your mother.   ❏
2 Ought you to be out of bed?   ❏
3 You'd better not call Jane while she is working.   ❏
4 I should better tidy my room.   ❏
5 You ought to send Olivia a thank-you card.   ❏
6 You don't should go to work if you are ill.   ❏

Exercise 2

Choose the correct word or words.

1 You really **ought not / should not** to eat so much chocolate.
2 If you have problems with maths, you **should / better** talk to your teacher.
3 I'd **better not / better not to** stay much longer.
4 **Ought we / Should we** to knock if the door is closed?
5 There's always a long queue, so you'd **ought / better** get there early.
6 **Should / Ought** I take her some flowers?

Exercise 3

Are the bold words correct or incorrect in the sentences?

1 I think you should **to** ❏ call the police.
2 You really **oughtn't** ❏ to read her diary.
3 You **should** ❏ better get a map from the tourist office.
4 **Ought** ❏ we to wear coats?
5 Visitors **shouldn't** ❏ take food into the bedrooms.
6 I think you **better** ❏ not go to work today.

Exercise 4

Put the correct words in each gap.

| 'd better not try | ought to ask | shouldn't go | should rest |
| ought to wear | shouldn't do |

Dear Diana

I heard that you fell off your bike. You really ¹_____ so fast on it, and I told

you that you ²_____ a helmet! You are lucky that you only hurt your arm.

You ³_____ your arm for a couple of weeks, but then you

⁴_____ the doctor for some exercises, so that it doesn't get too weak. You

⁵_____ too much though, and you ⁶_____ to ride

your bike until your arm's completely better.

Love

Michelle

Exercise 5

Complete the sentences by writing one word in each gap.

1 I'd _____ hurry up, or I'll be late for work again!

2 It's nearly dinner time – you'd better _____ eat any more crisps or you won't be hungry.

3 When that red light is on, you should _____ touch the machine because it's very hot.

4 You really ought not _____ miss the new film we saw last night.

5 I think I _____ better say sorry to Martha for shouting at her.

6 _____ I to invite your cousin David to my party?

Exercise 6

Choose the correct word or words.

Mum gets angry

You and your sister really ¹**should / ought** to do more to help at home! At your age, you ²**shouldn't / better not** still expect me to do everything for you. For a start, you ³**ought / should** make your own beds in the morning, and clear up your dirty clothes. In fact, you ⁴**ought / should** to do your own washing and ironing by now. And you'd ⁵**oughtn't / better not** let me find any more dirty plates and cups in your bedrooms!

If you don't want me to stop your pocket money, you'd ⁶**better / should** start helping me!

20

Modal verbs (4)

Making and responding to offers and promises

will, shall

In this unit you learn about using **will** and **shall** to make and respond to offers and promises.

Dan, Ben and Tom are getting ready for a camping trip.

Dan: I'll go and buy some food. Shall I get the train tickets too?

Ben: Yes, good idea. I'll give you the money when you get back. I'll check the tent is OK. Will you help me, Tom?

Tom: OK, and then I'll phone the campsite. If we haven't booked it, they won't let us stay.

Camping Trip	
food	Dan
train tickets	Dan
check tent	Ben and Tom
phone campsite	Tom

You use **will** when you offer or promise to do something.

I'll go and buy some food.
I'll pay you when you get back.

You can also use **Shall I …? / Shall we …?** to offer to do something.

> *Shall I get the train tickets?*

To ask if someone is going to do something you can use **Will you …?**

> *Will you help me?*

You can use **won't** about people or animals to show they don't want to do something.

> *They won't let us stay at the campsite.*
> *I've given the cats their food but they won't eat it.*

You can also use **won't** to talk about machines that don't work.

> *My computer still won't start properly. I think I need a new one.*

Exercise 1

Put the correct word in each gap.

| would | will | come | shall | 'll help | won't | make |

Sarah goes shopping

Karl: Hi Sarah. Where are you going?

Sarah: I want to go shopping but my car ¹_____ start. Stupid thing!

Karl: ²_____ you like a lift?

Sarah: Oh, thanks very much. I've got to get a lot of food and drink because of my party tomorrow.

Karl: I ³_____ you if you like. ⁴_____ Greg be at the party?

Sarah: No, he won't ⁵_____. He says he's too shy.

Karl: That's a shame. ⁶_____ I call him and ask him to come with me?

Sarah: Yes, please. Tell him I'll ⁷_____ sure everyone is friendly to him!

Exercise 2

Choose the correct word.

1 I've tried and tried, but this key **won't / shan't** fit in the lock.
2 These boxes are very heavy. **Shall / Will** you help me carry them?
3 I've asked Mum to lend me some money, but I don't know if she **won't / will**.
4 If your clothes **won't / will** fit in that suitcase, you can use this bigger one.
5 You **will / shall** tell me all about your trip, won't you?
6 **Shall / Will** we do the washing-up for you?

Exercise 3

Match the sentence halves.

1 What shall I do if
2 Shall we go with you
3 I don't think Charles
4 I will never
5 My dog won't come
6 I promise that I'll

a will lend us any more money.
b lie to you again.
c when I call him.
d to the hospital?
e the computer won't work?
f be back by 6.

Exercise 4

Put each sentence into the correct order.

1 cook the / everyone tonight / shall I / dinner for / ?

_____

2 won't tell / is laughing / my brother / me why he / .

_____

3 think Dad / to the airport / do you / take me / will / ?

_____

4 write to / says he / day / Ben / will / Emma every / .

_____

5 lid / come / off / this / won't / jar's / .

_____

6 hard work for / 'll / of the / do most / he / you / .

_____

Exercise 5

Which sentences are correct?

1 Shall I call a taxi for you?   ❏
2 This window won't open.   ❏
3 Shall you help me carry these cases, please?   ❏
4 My parents won't let me borrow their car.   ❏
5 Will I help you with your essay?   ❏
6 I won't never leave you.   ❏

Exercise 6

Are the bold words correct or incorrect in the sentences?

1 I've asked twice, but she **won't** ❏ come to the party.
2 Ben says he **will** ❏ do the cooking.
3 **Shall** ❏ we help you with the washing-up?
4 She says she **won't** ❏ never forget me.
5 My new printer **shall** ❏ print on both sides of the paper.
6 The horses **won't** ❏ go in the truck.

21

Passive

Passive verbs in the present and past

is, are, was, were + past participle

In this unit you learn about using the passive to talk about actions in the past and present.

You form the passive with the verb **be** and the past participle (e.g. **made**, **told**).

Passive be + past participle		
Present simple	**Past simple**	**Present perfect**
Paper is made from wood.	The building was completed in 1853.	All the rooms have just been painted.
A: When is the room cleaned? B: Every day.	A: When was the film made? B: In 2012.	A: Have you been served yet? B: No, I'm still waiting.
Pineapples aren't grown in Scotland.	His homework wasn't done very well.	The book hasn't been written yet.

You often use the passive when the object of the verb is more important than the subject, so

They completed the building in 1853.

becomes

*The building **was completed** in 1853.*

In passive sentences, you use **by** before the person or thing that causes the action (the agent).

*J.K. Rowling **wrote** the Harry Potter books.* (active)
*The Harry Potter books **were written by** J.K. Rowling.* (passive)

If you do not know who the agent is, or it is clear who it is, you don't need to use it.

*His wallet **was stolen** (by someone) while he was on holiday.*
*Letters **are delivered** (by the postman) every morning.*

> *Remember!*
>
> Most past participles end in **-ed**. Some are irregular:
>
> *do → done*
> *eat → eaten*
> *drive → driven*
> *write → written*
> *see → seen*
> *read → read*

Exercise 1

Match the sentences with the pictures.

1 The letters are collected twice a day.

a

2 Food is served from 7 to 10 p.m.

b

3 The grass is cut once a week.

c

4 Staff are paid at the end of the week.

d

5 The floor is cleaned every evening.

e

6 The towels are changed every morning.

f

Exercise 2

Write the past participle of the verb in brackets to complete each sentence.

1 Karen was _____ (give) a scarf for her birthday.

2 Were you _____ (take) to the station by taxi?

3 All the cake was _____ (eat) at the party.

4 I was late for work, so the beds weren't _____ (make) before I left.

5 Roberto wasn't _____ (tell) about the meeting.

6 The washing-up wasn't _____ (do) last night, so I'll do it now.

Exercise 3

Choose the correct word.

1 Hamid **was / were** given some money for his birthday.

2 We **were / was** taken to the airport by taxi.

3 I **were / was** invited to Linda's wedding.

4 **Was / Were** the windows cleaned yesterday?

5 What job **were / was** Stacey offered?

6 We **weren't / wasn't** paid last week.

Exercise 4

Complete the sentences by writing one word in each gap.

served | Has | been | haven't | Have | hasn't

1 _____ you been paid yet?

2 The tables _____ been cleaned yet. I'll clean them now.

3 I've come to collect my car. _____ it been fixed yet?

4 The letters have just _____ collected from the post box.

5 Those customers haven't been _____ yet, so I'd better serve them now.

6 That house is still empty – it _____ been lived in for years.

Exercise 5

Complete the sentences by writing one word in each gap.

was | were | is | has | Have | are

1 Dan and Sophie _____ both given new jobs last week.

2 The café tables _____ cleaned every evening, after customers go home.

3 Ahmad _____ been invited to the birthday meal, so he's happy.

4 _____ you been told the news?

5 On her birthday, Elena _____ always given flowers by her boyfriend.

6 Jake's bike _____ stolen from outside the college.

Exercise 6

Write the missing words in sentence B so that it means the same as sentence A.

1 **A** My parents gave us a new car.

  B We were _____ a new car by my parents.

2 **A** Sven's boss has offered him more money.

  B Sven has _____ offered more money by his boss.

3 **A** Someone stole Marta's mobile last week.

  B Marta's mobile was _____ last week.

4 **A** We keep all the pots in this cupboard.

  B All the pots are _____ in this cupboard.

5 **A** Someone has eaten all the sandwiches!

  B All the sandwiches _____ been eaten!

6 **A** Someone cleans the windows here once a month.

  B The windows are _____ here once a month.

22

Question tags

Using question tags with present and past meanings

isn't it?, didn't you?

In this unit you learn about using and forming question tags. You also learn about using short answers to yes/no questions.

A woman is interviewing a man for a job. Try to match the woman's questions with the man's answers.

1 Come and sit down. It's a nice day today, isn't it?

2 Now, let me see. You work at MBS now, don't you?

3 And you've been there for five years, haven't you?

4 And before that you worked at GHK, didn't you?

5 You can drive, can't you?

a Yes, I have.

b Yes, I do.

c Yes, it is.

d No, I can't.

e Yes, I did.

Answers: 1c 2b 3a 4e 5d

Question tags

You use question tags to check if something is true or if someone agrees with you.

*You were born in London, **weren't you**?*
*The weather's been bad this week, **hasn't it**?*

Short answers with yes/no questions

It is more polite to give a short answer to a yes/no question than simply saying **yes** or **no**.

A: Do you like living here?
*B: **Yes, I do.***

A: Have you seen the film yet?
*B: **No, I haven't.***

A: You don't like him, do you?
*B: **Yes, I do.***

Forming question tags and short answers

With the verb **be** and auxiliary and modal verbs (**be**, **have**, **will**, **can**, **could**, **must**, **should**, etc.) you form the question tag and short answer with the same verb.

Main verb	Question tag	Example	Short answer
it is	isn't it?	It's a nice day today, isn't it?	Yes, it is.
she can't	can she?	She can't drive, can she?	No, she can't.
you should	shouldn't you?	You should tell them, shouldn't you?	Yes, I should.
he has worked	hasn't he?	He's worked there a long time, hasn't he?	Yes, he has.
they were eating	weren't they?	They were eating pizza last night, weren't they?	Yes, they were.
it was built	wasn't it?	It was built in 1970, wasn't it?	Yes, it was.
I'll see	won't I?	I'll see you later, won't I?	Yes, you will.

Remember!

If the main verb is positive, the question tag is negative:
*They **aren't** coming, **are they**?*

If the main verb is negative, the question tag is positive:
*You **haven't** worked here long, **have you**?*

With all other verbs, you form the question tag and short answer with **do**.

Main verb	Question tag	Example	Short answer
you live	don't you?	You live in Germany, don't you?	Yes, I do.
she likes	doesn't she?	She likes pasta, doesn't she?	Yes, she does.
he swam	didn't he?	He swam from England to France, didn't he?	Yes, he did.
we visited	didn't we	We visited them last year, didn't we?	Yes, we did.

Exercise 1

Choose the correct phrase.

1 You enjoy playing hockey, **doesn't it / don't you**?

2 It hasn't rained for nearly a month, **did it / has it**?

3 There aren't any more tomatoes in the fridge, **is there / are there**?

4 Roger went to the same school as you, **didn't he / didn't you**?

5 Your parents have been living in that house for a long time, **haven't they / didn't they**?

6 You were born in France, **didn't you / weren't you**?

Exercise 2

Match the sentence halves.

1 Stephen hasn't changed his job,

2 There wasn't anything to do,

3 Your father isn't very good at tennis,

4 Maggie and Tom gave each of their grandchildren a bicycle,

5 There were lots of people at the festival,

6 The people you work with were very friendly when you started,

a is he?

b weren't they?

c has he?

d weren't there?

e didn't they?

f was there?

Exercise 3

Complete the sentences by writing a phrase in each gap.

1 It's very warm today, _____?

2 You've been to Sydney, _____?

3 Your mother's books have been sold, _____?

4 You don't like bananas, _____?

5 Your sister is watching a film, _____?

6 It doesn't often snow here, _____?

Exercise 4

Are the bold words correct or incorrect in the sentences?

1 Some people don't like using computers, **do they** ☐?

2 The Internet was developed in the 1960s, **wasn't it** ☐?

3 Most people send emails these days, **don't they** ☐?

4 Bill Gates and Paul Allen set up Microsoft in 1975, **didn't they** ☐?

5 There are lots of things that can be done with the computer, **aren't they** ☐?

6 Your laptop hasn't been scanned since last week, **is it** ☐?

Exercise 5

Write the short answers to the questions using the information in brackets, as shown.

1 Are there two major football teams in Manchester? _____*Yes, there are.*_____ (Yes)

2 Has David Beckham ever played for Manchester City? _____ (No)

3 Was Manchester United the first team to win the Premier League, FA Cup and UEFA Champions League in the same season? _____ (Yes)

4 Has Manchester United always had that name? _____ (No)

5 Have you ever been to a Manchester United match? _____ (Yes)

6 When you saw Manchester United play, were there many people watching? _____ (Yes)

23

Verbs not normally used in continuous forms

think, believe, know, understand, like, hate, have, feel, smell, taste, etc.

In this unit you learn about verbs that you do not usually use in continuous forms.

There are a few kinds of verb that you do not usually use in continuous forms. These are verbs related to

- thoughts, for example **think**, **believe**, **know** and **understand**:

    A: What **do you think of** the new James Bond film? B: It's fantastic.
    I **don't believe** you. It can't be true.
    I **didn't understand** the last part. Can you explain it again?

- likes and dislikes, e.g. **like**, **hate**, **prefer**:

    I really **like** that new restaurant.
    I **prefer** hot drinks to cold drinks.

- possessions, for example **have**, **own** and **belong to**:

    This ring **belonged** to my grandmother.
    She doesn't **have** much money.

- senses, for example **feel**, **smell**, **taste** and **sound**:

    This chicken **tastes** good.
    Have you heard their new CD? It **sounds** really good.

Some of these verbs do have continuous forms when they have a different meaning

- verbs describing senses:

> They smell lovely!

*She's **smelling** the flowers.*

> It tastes delicious!

*He's **tasting** the soup.*

● **have** and **think**

have	= to possess	He has two showers in his house.
	other meanings	A: Where's Anthony? B: He's having a shower. I'm having a bad day. My computer's broken and my car won't start.
think	= to believe / have an opinion	I think my car is faster than yours.
	other meanings	I'm thinking of buying a new car. She was thinking about her last holiday.

Exercise 1

Match the sentence halves.

1 The chef is tasting   **a** why he's having so many problems with his computer.

2 Do you believe   **b** all the scarves to find the softest one.

3 Jim doesn't really understand   **c** better than any I've ever had.

4 Does Marian own   **d** the food to make sure it's perfect.

5 This soup tastes   **e** what Laurel told you?

6 Anna is feeling   **f** the flat where she lives?

Exercise 2

Which sentences are correct?

1 Frank feels tired, so he's gone to bed.   ❑

2 I'm knowing exactly how you feel.   ❑

3 Are you seeing what I mean?   ❑

4 Do you think it's going to be sunny tomorrow?   ❑

5 Are you seeing the doctor today?   ❑

6 Our new car was costing nearly £10,000.   ❑

Exercise 3

Complete the sentences by writing a word or phrase in each gap.

are smelling	think	are knowing	smell	are feeling
are thinking	know	belong		

1 Patrick and Carol _____ happy because they've just had a baby.

2 A lot of people _____ where I live.

3 Most of my friends _____ of going to college next year.

4 Fresh bread and coffee both _____ delicious.

5 My parents _____ I should accept the job offer.

6 Those DVDs _____ to me.

Exercise 4

Are the bold words correct or incorrect in the sentences?

1 Your dogs **are seeming** ❏ quite friendly.
2 Why **are you tasting** ❏ the soup?
3 Don't you think this room **feels** ❏ very cold?
4 The children were watching the plane so they **weren't thinking** ❏ about their lesson.
5 Listen! **Are you hearing** ❏ that strange noise upstairs?
6 Some of the staff in this shop **don't seem** ❏ to know anything about the products.

Exercise 5

Are the bold words correct or incorrect in this text?

Hi Ruth!

You asked me to suggest somewhere to go on holiday. Well, how about Corsica? **You're liking** ❏ the sea, and Corsica is an island. There **are** ❏ also lots of mountains. I've found a hotel which **is having** ❏ a swimming pool and entertainment, and it **looks** ❏ very nice. In fact, **I'm thinking** ❏ of going there myself. Corsica is part of France, but I know **you're understanding** ❏ French. Tell me what you decide.

Love

Tommy

Exercise 6

Write the correct present tense form of the verb in brackets to complete each sentence.

1 Do you see what that man is doing now? He _____ (taste) the cheese before he buys it.
2 I _____ (not understand) what's wrong with this car.
3 Sam _____ (not think) about his work today, so he's making lots of mistakes.
4 I'm sure everyone _____ (know) where New York is.
5 Cathy _____ (not like) fish, so she's having an omelette instead.
6 I _____ (not believe) everything I read on the Internet.

24

Verbs followed by two objects

verb + object + verb

In this unit you learn about verbs which are followed by the infinitive. You also learn about verbs followed by an indirect and direct object.

Verb + object + infinitive (without *to*)

Make and **let**

*My mum **made** my dad do the washing-up. (He had no choice. He had to do the washing-up.)*

*She **let** me hold the baby. (She gave me permission to hold the baby.)*

Verb + object + infinitive (with *to*)

	Verb	+ object	+ *to* + *infinitive*
want	I really want	you	to read this magazine.
would like	Would you like	John	to make some coffee?
help	She helped	my sister	to do her homework.
ask	Can you ask	him	to text me?
teach	He's teaching	me	to speak Japanese.
expect	I expect	him	to phone this evening.

> *Remember!*
> You can use **help** with or without **to**.
> *I helped her **(to)** choose a dress for the party.*

Verb + indirect object + direct object

Some verbs, for example **tell**, **ask**, **take** and **give** can be followed by an indirect and direct object:

*My brother told **my sister a story**.*

In this sentence, **story** is the direct object and **sister** is the indirect object.

*She always asks **me lots of questions**.*
*I want to give **my Mum a present**.*

> ### Remember!
>
> If the indirect object comes after the direct object, you need to put **to** before it:
>
> *My brother told a story **to my sister**.*
> *I want to give a present **to my Mum**.*

Exercise 1

Find the wrong or extra word in each sentence, as shown.

1 Don't let me ~~it~~ forget to buy some stamps at the post office.

2 Stephanie would like that you to play tennis with her this afternoon.

3 Do you think you can make the printer to start working again?

4 Shall we give to Helen a bunch of flowers?

5 Danny wants that his friends to visit him while he's in hospital.

6 The visitors took for Tom a box of chocolates.

Exercise 2

Decide if the pairs of sentences have the same meaning.

1 **A** Let me help you carry your books upstairs.
  B Let me help you to carry your books upstairs. ☐

2 **A** I'd like you to cook dinner for Trudy, please.
  B Trudy wants you to cook dinner for me. ☐

3 **A** I forgot to give the college my email address.
  B I forgot to give my email address to the college. ☐

4 **A** I didn't want her to see the film. ☐
  B I didn't make her see the film.

5 **A** When I was about 12, my parents let me go out on my own.
  B When I was about 12, my parents made me go out on my own. ☐

Exercise 3

Choose the correct word.

1 The whole class agreed to **let / help / give** the teacher a present.

2 Nobody **helped / made / let** the man to look for his missing laptop.

3 My father **let / taught / made** me to drive.

4 We **would like / will let / hope** the work to finish in the next few days.

5 The bookshop **hopes / expects / thinks** sales of cookery books to rise.

Exercise 4

Choose the correct word or phrase.

Johnny's parents were delighted when he was born, and while he was growing up they never made him ¹**to do / do** anything he didn't want ²**do / to do**. For example, if he didn't want ³**that he eat / to eat** particular types of food, he didn't eat them. And they let him ⁴**eat / to eat** as many sweets as he wanted to. The result was that whenever they asked ⁵**that he was / him to be** polite to visitors, for example, he wasn't – unless the visitors gave ⁶**him / to him** some sweets! Johnny was a spoilt child.

Exercise 5

Are the bold words correct or incorrect in the sentences?

1 Peter would like all his friends **came** ☐ to his birthday party next Saturday.

2 He hopes a few people will go to the party early, to help him **cook** ☐ some food.

3 If you can go early, please let Peter **to know** ☐ as soon as possible.

4 Please don't bring **to him** ☐ a present.

5 The party will start at 8 p.m., and he expects it **to end** ☐ about midnight.

6 Peter wants everyone **to have** ☐ a good time.

Exercise 6

Which sentences are correct?

1 Don't let the cat eat our lunch! ☐

2 I'd like some of you wait outside the room for a few minutes. ☐

3 I helped my brother carry the luggage to his car. ☐

4 I'd never make you to eat something you don't like. ☐

5 Do you want me tell you the answers? ☐

6 Anderson's goal helped the team to win their first football match of the season. ☐

25

Pronouns and adjectives

other, another, one/s

In this unit you learn ways of using **other** and **another** as adjectives and pronouns.

Other used as an adjective

You use **other** as an adjective before a singular or plural noun

- with **the**:

   *This room is quite small. **The other** room is much bigger.*
   ***The other** shops are on the second floor.*

- with expressions of quantity (**some**, **any**, **a few**, etc.):

   *I've got **some other** DVDs at home. I'll bring them tomorrow.*
   *Have you got **any other** ideas?*

- with possessive adjectives (**my**, **his**, **your**, etc.):

   *I lost **my other** shoes so I'm wearing these old ones.*

Another used as an adjective

You use **another**

- before a singular countable noun to mean **one more**:

   *Would you like **another** cup of coffee?*
   *They had **another** house in the mountains.*

- before numbers:

   *We're going to stay there for **another** three weeks. (= three more weeks)*

Other and *another* before *one/ones*

   *My phone is very old. I'm going to get **another one**. (= another phone)*
   *I quite liked his new film but I think his **other ones** were much better. (= other films)*

Others and *another* as pronouns

You can use **others** and **another** as pronouns. The meaning is the same as **another one** and **other ones**.

   *I really liked that ice cream. I'm going to get **another**.*

   A: Have we eaten all the apples?
   *B: No, there are some **others** in the kitchen.*

   *A: Where are the **others**?*
   B: They're watching TV.

> *Remember!*
>
> You usually put **the**, a quantity word like **some** or **any**, a number or a possessive adjective (**my**, **his**, **your**, etc.) before **others**.
>
> *We've watched all the DVDs. There aren't **any others** to watch.*

Exercise 1

Match the two parts.

1 That coffee was lovely, Molly!

2 What a beautiful photo!

3 I bought two dresses – this one I'm wearing and a red one.

4 She's written loads of books and I've only read one of them.

5 She's written two books and I've read one of them. It was very good.

6 Christopher has just bought another car.

a I can lend you some of her other ones, if you like.

b Would you like to borrow the other one? I finished it last week.

c Good! Would you like another one?

d Really? Hasn't he already got two?

e That looks lovely on you. Can I see the other one?

f Thank you! Would you like to see the others?

Exercise 2

For each question, tick the correct answer.

1 Would you like
❑ other coffee?
❑ another coffee?

2 I've read that book. Have you got
❑ any other?
❑ any others?

3 My glass was dirty so I asked for
❑ another one.
❑ some other.

4 These jeans are a bit too big. Are there any
❑ other one?
❑ other ones?

5 He had one slice of cake and then
❑ some other.
❑ another.

Exercise 3

Choose the correct word.

1 There were some **other / others** people waiting.

2 Could I have **other / another** glass of water, please?

3 I don't like those colours. Are there any **other / others**?

4 There were problems with the weather in **another / other** countries too.

5 There was **another / other** part of the film that I didn't understand.

6 I'm going to one party tonight and **other / another** one tomorrow night.

Exercise 4

Put each sentence into the correct order.

1 she / does / any / other / have / friends / ? _____

2 another / would / like / drink / you / ? _____

3 had / few / a / other / we / problems / . _____

4 any / are / other / cakes / there / ? _____

5 another / shall / try / café / we / ? _____

6 you / the / could / others / tell / ? _____

Exercise 5

Complete the sentences by writing one word in each gap.

| other | any | another | others | one | the |

1 I didn't like the meal in the hotel but I liked the _____ meal that we had in the restaurant.

2 I already have this book. Do you have _____ other books on English grammar?

3 She showed me two apartments. One was too small and _____ other was too big.

4 That coffee was so good, Melissa! Could I have _____, please?

5 It was such a small coffee. Would you like another _____?

6 I've seen all these films. Do you have any _____?

Exercise 6

Put the correct word in each gap.

| other | others | any | one | another | ones |

I was looking for a smart jacket so I asked the girl who worked in the shop to help me. I didn't like the first jacket that she showed me, so I asked to see some ¹_____. She brought me two – a short, black one and ²_____ one which was dark red. The black one was too short and the ³_____ one was too long. I explained the problem and asked if she had ⁴_____ others. She then showed me another ⁵_____ which was far too expensive. I think I'm going to try the shops in Green Street. Do you know any other ⁶_____ where I might find a nice jacket?

26

Relative pronouns and reflexive pronouns

who, which, that; myself, yourself

In this unit you learn about relative clauses with **who**, **which** and **that**. You also learn to use reflexive pronouns (**myself**, **yourself**, etc.).

Relative clauses

You use relative clauses to say exactly who or what you are talking about.

I've got two brothers. One lives in Paris and the other lives in New York.

The brother **who lives in Paris** loves football.

The brother **who lives in New York** plays the guitar.

You use **who**, **which** or **that** before a relative clause.

Relative pronoun	For	Example
who or **that**	people	That's the girl who/that works in the post office.
which or **that**	things	I saw a house which/that looked very old.

In these sentences, the relative pronoun is the subject of the relative clause.

The relative pronoun can also be the object of the relative clause.

Look at these two sentences:

I wanted to buy a computer. It was very expensive.

You can make one sentence from these two sentences using **that**.

*The computer **that I wanted to buy** was very expensive.*

You can use **that** to talk about things or people.

I saw a girl. She was very pretty.
*The girl **that I saw** was very pretty.*

Reflexive pronouns

You can use a reflexive pronoun to show that you did something to yourself and not to another person or thing.

*She's teaching **herself** Japanese.*

*She's teaching **them** Japanese.*

Subject pronoun	Object pronoun	Reflexive pronoun
I	me	myself
you	you	yourself (singular) yourselves (plural)
he	him	himself
she	her	herself
it	it	itself
we	us	ourselves
they	them	themselves

These are some verbs that you often use with a reflexive pronoun.

cut	She cut herself while she was preparing the vegetables.
dry	We got out of the swimming pool and dried ourselves.
enjoy	They really enjoyed themselves at the concert.
help	Help yourself to more food.
hurt	Don't climb up there. You'll hurt yourself!
look after	He's old enough to look after himself.

You also use reflexive pronouns to show that you can do something without help.

*I drove the car **myself**.*
*These cakes are really nice. Did you make them **yourself**?*

You can use **by himself/themselves**, etc. to mean **alone**.

A: Did you go to the cinema with your sister?
*B: No, I went **by myself**.*

each other

Jane emails Sunil. Sunil emails Jane.
*They email **each other**.*

Exercise 1

Which sentences are correct?

1 A true friend is someone who helps you when you have a problem. ❏

2 The first car that I bought was 30 years old. ❏

3 I know a lot of the people which live in my town. ❏

4 Physics is the only subject that I found difficult at school. ❏

5 Could you pass me the cup which is on the table behind you, please? ❏

6 This is the laptop who I'm having a problem with. ❏

Exercise 2

Complete the sentences by writing one word in each gap.

| himself | herself | another | yourselves | other | others |
| each | ourselves | another | | | |

1 Kate and her brother gave each _____ watches as a birthday present.

2 If you're hungry, please help _____ to some food.

3 Helen's parents looked at one _____ and smiled.

4 Is your son old enough to go out by _____?

5 We both asked _____ the same question.

6 It took us quite a long time to get to know _____ other.

Exercise 3

Match the sentence halves.

1 My sister baked this bread   **a** myself.

2 I often go for a walk by   **b** himself.

3 Sarah, I'm not sure you wrote this story   **c** herself.

4 My uncle and aunt are very old but they can look after   **d** yourselves.

5 I hope you and your wife enjoyed   **e** yourself.

6 The man lives by   **f** themselves.

Exercise 4

Complete the sentences by writing one word in each gap.

themselves	yourselves	himself	yourself	itself	ourselves	
myself	herself					

1 Philip, you don't know anything about it – you said so _____.

2 Gary and Karen are old enough to go to school by _____.

3 Sharon hurt _____ when she tried to move the heavy cupboard.

4 We never buy vegetables – we grow all our vegetables _____.

5 Now, children, be careful when you cut up your food – you might cut _____.

6 The company wants to make a car that can drive by _____.

Exercise 5

Decide if the pairs of sentences have the same meaning.

1 **A** Terry will look after him.
  B Terry will look after himself. ☐

2 **A** Kelly sent an email to Bill and Bill sent an email to Kelly about the party.
  B Kelly and Bill sent each other emails about the party. ☐

3 **A** I'll spend the money which I save on my next holiday.
  B I'll spend the money that I save on my next holiday. ☐

4 **A** I'd like you to take some photographs of me.
  B I'd like to take some photographs of myself. ☐

5 **A** The person that I spend most time with is Jane.
  B Jane is the person who I spend most time with. ☐

Exercise 6

Write the missing words in sentence B so that it means the same as sentence A.

1 A Patsy knows Jim and Jim knows Patsy quite well.

  B Patsy and Jim know _____ other quite well.

2 A We all had a good time at the concert yesterday evening.

  B We all enjoyed _____ at the concert yesterday evening.

3 A I speak German, although I've never had any lessons.

  B I've taught _____ to speak German.

4 A Nobody that lives in my town wants the new road to be built.

  B Nobody _____ lives in my town wants the new road to be built.

Exercise 7

Put the correct word in each gap.

| one | who | you | yourself | myself | which | each |

Hi Pete!

You asked me about clothes for your new job. I think you should buy ¹_____ some new shirts. The shirts ²_____ you usually wear are really old! I know you and Hazel usually give ³_____ other books or DVDs as presents, but why not ask her to give ⁴_____ a shirt? And don't wait for your birthday!

You also asked if I need help with painting my living room. It's very kind of you, but I think I can do it ⁵_____, with some help from the man ⁶_____ lives next door. We're going to start tomorrow.

Good luck with the new job!

Scott

27

Phrasal verbs

Common phrasal verbs in the past and present (*look after, put away, get up*)

In this unit you learn the meaning of some common phrasal verbs.

Many common verbs are used in phrasal verbs:

Look

look after	I'm going to the shops. Can you **look after** the children?
look up	I always **look up** new words in the dictionary.
look for	Can you help me **look for** my keys? I've lost them.

Put

put away	It's time for lunch now. **Put away** your books.
put on	It's cold outside. Make sure you **put on** a coat.
put off	Don't **put off** your homework until tomorrow.

Get

get up	I usually **get up** late on Sundays.
get in	**Get in** here quickly. It's cold outside.
get out of	I'll **get out of** the car at the station.

Other phrasal verbs

switch on/off	Make sure you **switch off** the lights before you leave.
turn on/off	The programme is about to start. **Turn on** the TV.
make up	I **made up** the story. It wasn't true.
run out of	Go to the garage. You don't want to **run out of** petrol.
fill in	To get a passport you have to **fill in** a long form.
find out	I'll **find out** the answer on the Internet.

Remember!

With many phrasal verbs, the object pronoun (**it/them/us,** etc.) goes between the verb and **on/off/out,** etc.

*Do your homework today. Don't put **it** off until tomorrow.*
*There's a problem with my computer. I can't switch **it** on.*

Exercise 1

Match the sentences with the pictures.

1 He's run out of petrol. **a**

2 He's looking up a word. **b**

3 He's filling in a form. **c**

4 He's just got up. **d**

5 He's looking for his book. **e**

6 He's looking after his children. **f**

Exercise 2

Match the sentence halves.

1 You often need to fill in
2 Jack looks after his
3 Oh no! We've run out of
4 Ben always gets up
5 Izzy is looking for her
6 I need to look up

a coffee – I'll have to have tea.
b a form to get a job.
c three sons very well.
d early in the morning.
e car keys.
f a phone number on the Internet.

Exercise 3

For each question, tick the correct answer.

1 I was cold, so I found my sweater and put it
- ☐ off.
- ☐ away.
- ☐ on.

2 I couldn't remember how to spell his name so I
- ☐ switched it off.
- ☐ made it up.
- ☐ filled it in.

3 Susanna didn't know anything about Belgium so she went on the Internet and
- ☐ found out.
- ☐ looked for.
- ☐ turned on.

4 When you've finished on the computer,
- ☐ make it up.
- ☐ switch it off.
- ☐ put it on.

5 Jeff drove to his house, stopped and
- ☐ got out of his car.
- ☐ put off his car.
- ☐ looked for his car.

6 I didn't want to tell my friend the bad news, so I
- ☐ looked after it.
- ☐ put it off.
- ☐ ran out of it.

Exercise 4

Put each sentence into the correct order.

1 switched / the / I / light / off / .

_____

2 Gemma / clothes / puts / her / cupboard / the / away in / .

_____

3 made up / story / a / for / Harry / children / his / .

_____

4 found / John / information / Internet / on / the / out some / .

_____

5 coat / put / on in / Jill / her / the hall / .

_____

6 children / looking / is / my / sister / after / my two / .

_____

Exercise 5

Complete the sentences by writing one word in each gap.

off | out | after | in | away | up

1 Leo is a good son: he looks _____ his parents now that they're old.
2 You need to fill _____ this form if you want the job.
3 I always put _____ the things that I don't like doing.
4 I'm going to the shops because we've run _____ of bread.
5 I usually get _____ at 7 a.m. on school days and leave home at 8.
6 I need to put _____ the clean cups and plates in the kitchen.

Exercise 6

Choose the correct word or words.

1 I need to look **after / up** a word in the dictionary.
2 Please turn **on / off** the light because I can't see.
3 I need to get **out of / up** early tomorrow morning.
4 If you're cold, put **on / off** your sweater.
5 James had to look **up / for** his keys before he left.
6 Sarah stopped the car and switched **on / off** the engine.

28

Requests, offers and invitations

let me, shall, would you, can, could, may

In this unit you learn ways of making and responding to offers, invitations and requests.

Offering

> Let me help you.

You can use these phrases to offer to do things.

Let me carry your suitcase.	Thanks.
Shall I go to the shops with you?	Thank you.
Can I help you?	It's OK, thank you.
Do you need any more money?	No, I'm OK, thanks.

Inviting

You can invite people to do things with these phrases.

Would you like to see a film tomorrow?	Yes, I'd love to.
What about play**ing** tennis this afternoon?	Thanks, but I'm going shopping.
Shall we go for a walk?	No, I'm sorry. I'm too tired.

Requesting

To make requests you can use these phrases

- to ask someone to do something:

Can you open the window, please?	Yes, of course.
Could you tell me the time?	I'm sorry, I haven't got a watch.
Would you mind turn**ing** the TV down, please? It's very loud.	Not at all. (= I don't mind and I will do what you request)

● to ask if you can do something:

Can I leave early today, please?	No, I'm sorry. We're very busy.
Could I borrow your laptop?	Yes, of course.
May I ask you a question?	Of course.

May and **could** are more polite than **can**.

> *Remember!*
>
> Most of the phrases are followed by the infinitive:
> *Can I **help** you?*
> But **would you mind** and **what about** are followed by *-ing*.
> ***Would you mind** closing the window?*

Exercise 1

Match the two parts.

1 Would you like a drink?

2 Do you need anything else?

3 Shall I call a taxi for you?

4 Let me take your suitcase.

5 Would you mind turning your music off?

6 Can you show me how to play this game?

a The instructions are in the box.

b Thanks – it's really heavy!

c Do you have any extra pillows?

d Yes – can they pick us up in half an hour?

e No problem, sorry.

f I've just had one, thanks.

Exercise 2

For each question, tick the correct answer.

1 Can I .... at your new phone?
   ❑ look
   ❑ looking
   ❑ to look

2 Let me .... you a drink.
   ❑ getting
   ❑ get
   ❑ to get

3 Shall we .... that new app?
   ❑ to download
   ❑ downloading
   ❑ download

4 Would you like .... out for dinner tonight?
   ❑ to go
   ❑ go
   ❑ going

5 What about .... a film this weekend?
   ❑ see
   ❑ seeing
   ❑ to see

Exercise 3

Put a cross (X) by the questions or sentences that do not belong, as shown.

1 Requesting

May I use your phone?	☐
Not at all, any time.	☒
Could you close the door?	☐
What about pizza for lunch?	☐

2 Offering

Would you like some cheese?	☐
Would you mind giving me that file?	☐
Let's join the tennis club.	☐
Shall I book the holiday?	☐

3 Inviting

May I have another cake?	☐
Would you like to come round this evening?	☐
Let me take you out.	☐
Could you tell me the right answer, please?	☐

4 Accepting offers and invitations

Good idea.	☐
I'm sorry, I'm busy.	☐
Let's not do that.	☐
I'd love to.	☐

Exercise 4

Put the correct response in each gap.

No, thanks. I'm not hungry. | I'm sorry, I'm going out with Jim tonight. | Of course – but don't break it! | I've just sat down – maybe the next one! | Not at all. | Great. I can wear my new walking boots. | Thanks, but I'm busy on Saturday. | Sure. Here you are.

1 Do you want to dance to this song? _____

2 What about going hiking tomorrow? _____

3 Can I get you a sandwich? _____

4 Could you pass me that magazine? _____

5 Would you mind switching the light on? _____

6 Would you like to go camping this weekend? _____

7 Can I borrow your MP3 player? _____

8 Shall we go to the sports centre this evening? _____

Exercise 5

Put each sentence into the correct order.

1 can / help / your / project / with / I / you / ?

_____

2 towel for / do / need / beach / you / the / a / ?

_____

3 washing-up / let / do / me / the / .

_____

4 orange / about / what / a / glass / of / ?

_____

5 afternoon / you / like / would / come / swimming this / to / ?

_____

6 mind / you / me / helping / homework / with / my / would / ?

_____

Exercise 6

Decide if the pairs of sentences have the same meaning.

1 **A** Shall I do the shopping this week?
  B I don't want you to do the shopping this week. ❑

2 **A** Would you like to go swimming? ❑
  B I always enjoy swimming with you.

3 **A** What about seeing _Dinosaur_? ❑
  B Would you like to watch _Dinosaur_?

4 **A** Let me pay for lunch. ❑
  B I want to pay for lunch.

5 **A** Would you mind not smoking in here? ❑
  B It's OK for you to smoke in here.

6 **A** May I have a biscuit? ❑
  B Can I have a biscuit?

Exercise 7

Find the wrong or extra word in each sentence.

1 Shall I do shut the computer down?
2 What think about renting a car on holiday?
3 Can I do you anything to help?
4 Do you need for anything from the supermarket?
5 Would you like it some more pasta?
6 Can you please to close the door?

29

Agreeing, disagreeing and telling people what you want and need

In this unit you learn about how to agree and disagree, and how to tell people what you want or need and what they must do.

Agreeing and disagreeing

Martina	That was a brilliant film.
Anna	**I don't agree. I think** it was boring. **Don't you think that** the acting was bad?
Martina	No, not really. **It's true that** Jack Green was not very good in it but, **in my opinion**, it was the best film so far this year.
Anna	**I don't think so.**

I agree / don't agree that …	Do / Don't you agree that …?	I agree / don't agree (with you).
I think / don't think that …	Do / Don't you think that …?	I think / don't think so.
It's true that …	Is it true that …?	It's true / It's not true.
In my opinion …		

Expressing necessity and obligation

You can use these verbs to talk about what it is necessary or important for you to do or have.

- **need to** + verb; **need** + noun:

  *Can you be quiet. I **need to** finish this.*
  *It's late. **Do you need to** order a taxi?*
  *I **need** a new mobile phone. This one's really old.*

- **must** and **have to**:

  *I'm cooking dinner tonight. I **must** go to the shops.*

  *A: **Do you have to** leave now?*
  *B: Yes, I **have to** catch the next train.*

  *You **must** text me when you get there.*

> *Remember!*
>
> You use **mustn't** if it is important not to do something:
> *You **mustn't** make too much noise at the party.*
>
> You use **don't have to** if it is not necessary to do something:
> *She **doesn't have to** bring any food to the party.*
>
> See Unit 17 for more about **must** and **have to**.

Exercise 1

Decide if the pairs of sentences have the same meaning.

1 **A** In my opinion, children don't need mobile phones.
   B I don't think children need mobile phones. ☐

2 **A** It's true that if you work hard, you do well.
   B You don't have to work hard to be successful. ☐

3 **A** I agree with you.
   B I think the same as you. ☐

4 **A** Don't you think horses are nice?
   B I like horses – do you? ☐

5 **A** In my opinion, women drive better than men.
   B Women are not good drivers, nor are some men. ☐

Exercise 2

Match the phrases which mean the same.

1 It's true	**a** It isn't true
2 In my opinion	**b** She has to
3 I don't agree	**c** She believes
4 I need	**d** I don't have
5 It's her opinion	**e** I think
6 She needs to	**f** I agree

Exercise 3

Choose the correct word or words.

1 You **must / have to / need** not walk on the grass. It's wet.

2 Fluffy **has to / needs / must** a drink – he's very thirsty!

3 You **need / must / have** remember your sports kit tomorrow.

4 He **needs to / mustn't / has got** wear a hard hat for work.

5 Visitors **need / must / have** leave their shoes outside.

Exercise 4

Which sentences are correct?

1 I must a cup of tea! ❑

2 Students must not run inside school buildings. ❑

3 We have to catch the train in five minutes. ❑

4 Peter needs study harder to pass the exam. ❑

5 Victoria has to leave at 6 p.m. ❑

6 They must to hurry or they'll miss the bus. ❑

Exercise 5

Put the correct word in each gap.

| have | opinion | need | agree | true | must |

We had an interesting discussion in class today. We talked about how to become a good

sportsperson. I ¹_____ that it is important to get enough sleep and eat

well. Some people in the class think that people are born to be footballers or runners.

In my ²_____, you just ³_____ to work very hard. You don't

⁴_____ expensive trainers or the best tennis racket, but you ⁵_____

listen to your sports teacher. It's ⁶_____ that they give good advice.

Exercise 6

Put each sentence into the correct order.

1 agree / I / that / computer / game / easy / this / too / is / !

_____

2 opinion / are / the / boring / my / quite / in / pictures / .

_____

3 true / music's / the / it's / good / but / that / .

_____

4 new / games / need / get / to / I / some / .

_____

5 I'll / some / to / have / borrow / my friends / from / .

_____

6 need / I / phone / them / soon / to / .

_____

30

Suggesting, advising and saying that you're sure

In this unit you learn to say how certain you are about something, how to give advice and make suggestions.

Expressing certainty

 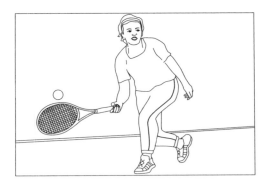

Dan	Look over there. **I'm sure** that's Maria playing tennis.
Sam	No, **it can't be**. I've just seen her at the library.
Dan	**Are you sure**?
Sam	Yes, **I'm sure**. I spoke to her there.
Dan	**It could be** her sister, Jo, then.
Sam	Of course, she's got a twin sister, hasn't she? **It must be** Jo.

Are you sure?			
It's certain	**It's possible**	**It's not certain**	**It's not possible**
I'm sure … / It must be …	It could be …	I'm not sure …	It can't be …

Giving advice

In Unit 19 you looked at ways of giving advice. Here are some other ways:

> **Gina** I need to get more exercise. What can I do?
>
> **Tim** **I think you should** join a gym.
>
> **Gina** It's too expensive.
>
> **Tim** **Why don't you** go for a run every day? That's free.

Making suggestions

Anna and Alex are planning their weekend. Look at the phrases they use to make suggestions.

> **Anna** **What shall we** do this weekend?
>
> **Alex** **What about going** to the new shopping centre?
>
> **Anna** I went there last week. **Why don't we** go to the park and play tennis?
>
> **Alex** That's a good idea. **Let's** go to that new café afterwards.
>
> **Anna** OK. **Shall** we ask Sara to come too?
>
> **Alex** Yes, **let's** do that.

Remember!

*Shall we **go** …?*
*Let's **go** …*
*Why don't we **go** …?*
BUT
*What about **going** …?*

Exercise 1

Match the sentences that mean the same.

1 I'm sure it's true.

2 I'm sure it isn't true.

3 I think it's important to tell the truth.

4 I don't know what's true.

5 Let's tell them the truth.

6 I think it might be true.

a Why don't we tell them the truth?

b It can't be true.

c I think we should tell the truth.

d It must be true.

e I think it could be true.

f I'm not sure what the truth is.

Exercise 2

For each question, tick the correct answer.

1 A: Who's that girl with Peter?
 B: ...., I haven't seen her before.
 ❑ I'm not sure
 ❑ It can't be
 ❑ It must be

2 A: .... go out for dinner?
 B: No, it's too expensive!
 ❑ Shall we
 ❑ What about
 ❑ Maybe

3 A: I've got toothache.
 B: .... go to the dentist.
 ❑ Why don't you
 ❑ Must
 ❑ You should

4 A: I'm bored.
 B: .... go shopping for shoes!
 ❑ What about
 ❑ Let's
 ❑ Could

5 A: Your brother has sent you a text.
 B: I guess he .... want a lift home.
 ❑ can't
 ❑ must
 ❑ should

Exercise 3

Choose the correct word or words.

1 **Why don't we / It could be / I'm sure** go skiing tomorrow?

2 This question is difficult. **I think / I can't / I'm not sure** what the answer is.

3 Petra hurt her hand yesterday. **What about / She should / Perhaps she** see a doctor.

4 Julia **must / can't be / could be** on holiday in Spain. I saw her in her office this morning.

5 **What about / Shall we / Let's** going away this weekend?

Exercise 4

Put the correct word in each gap.

| I'm sure | I think you should | can't be | could be | must | Let's | I'm sure |

Eva: I can't find my cat!

Ken: Oh, don't worry. ¹_____ she'll come back soon.

Eva: I don't know. She ²_____ up a tree!

Ken: When did you last see her?

Eva: Early this morning.

Ken: Well, she ³_____ far away.

Eva: ⁴_____ go and ask all the neighbours.

Ken: ⁵_____ wait a bit longer. ⁶_____ she'll come home for her dinner!

Exercise 5

Decide if the pairs of sentences have the same meaning.

1 **A** You can't be right.
   B I'm sure what you say is correct. ❏

2 **A** Why don't you try this book? It's great.
   B I think you should read this book. It's very good. ❏

3 **A** You must meet Ellie after school.
   B You could meet Ellie when she comes out of school. ❏

4 **A** Shall we have a picnic in the park?
   B Let's have a picnic in the park. ❏

5 **A** Jenny must be on holiday. ❏
   B I'm sure Jenny is on holiday.

Exercise 6

Are the bold words correct or incorrect in the sentences?

1 Steven must **be** ❏ about 40 years old.

2 Let's **we** ❏ go to the beach this afternoon.

3 I must **to** ❏ clean my car. It's very dirty!

4 What about **have** ❏ pizza for lunch?

5 I'm **not** ❏ sure what to do. I can't decide.

6 It **could** ❏ be too late to book a table. I'll ring the restaurant to find out.

Exercise 7

Which sentences are correct?

1 Let's go out tonight – it's very cold and I want to watch TV. ❏

2 Shall we play football this weekend? ❏

3 That woman can't be Sonia's daughter – she's too old. ❏

4 That red bike could be George's – his is blue. ❏

5 You must be hungry after eating all those sandwiches. ❏

6 Why don't you buy a new car – this one's so slow! ❏

Answer key

1 Present continuous, present simple and will

Exercise 1
1 are visiting *or* 're visiting
2 am seeing *or* 'm seeing
3 are going out
4 is swimming *or* 's swimming
5 are having *or* 're having
6 am taking *or* 'm taking

Exercise 2
1 will	4 am
2 does	5 are
3 be	6 is

Exercise 3
1 d	4 c
2 e	5 f
3 b	6 a

Exercise 4
1 does	4 doing
2 seeing	5 be
3 leaves	6 do

Exercise 5
1 f	4 e
2 a	5 c
3 b	6 d

Exercise 6
1 going	4 I'll
2 meeting	5 doing
3 won't	6 see

2 Present perfect

Exercise 1
1 a	4 b
2 e	5 d
3 c	6 f

Exercise 2
1 d	4 f
2 e	5 b
3 c	6 a

Exercise 3
1 ever	4 ever
2 never	5 ever
3 never	6 never

Exercise 4
1 d	4 e
2 b	5 f
3 c	6 a

Exercise 5
1 gone
2 been
3 been
4 gone
5 been
6 gone

Exercise 6
1 No	4 No
2 Yes	5 No
3 Yes	6 Yes

3 Prepositions

Exercise 1
1 a	4 c
2 f	5 d
3 b	6 e

Exercise 2
1 f	4 d
2 c	5 e
3 a	6 b

Exercise 3

1 to
2 to
3 at
4 with
5 to
6 at

Exercise 4

1 agree
2 ask
3 tell
4 watch
5 think
6 talk

Exercise 5

1 of
2 to
3 about
4 with
5 at
6 from

Exercise 6

1 No
2 No
3 Yes
4 No
5 Yes
6 Yes

4 A little and a few

Exercise 1

1 plenty
2 a few
3 couple
4 hardly
5 lot
6 little

Exercise 2

1 a few ✗
2 a few ✓
3 little ✗
4 lot of ✗
5 Several ✗
6 Plenty. ✓

Exercise 3

1 much
2 plenty
3 couple
4 several
5 hardly
6 a little

Exercise 4

1 f
2 a
3 e
4 b
5 d
6 c

Exercise 5

1 lots
2 little
3 few
4 a few
5 a little
6 Several

Exercise 6

1 Yes
2 No
3 No
4 Yes
5 Yes
6 No

5 Possessive pronouns

Exercise 1

1 d
2 f
3 b
4 e
5 a
6 c

Exercise 2

1 his
2 mine
3 theirs
4 yours
5 hers
6 ours

Exercise 3

1 c
2 a
3 d
4 f
5 e
6 b

Exercise 4

1 mine
2 yours
3 hers
4 ours
5 his
6 theirs

Exercise 5

1 hers
2 his
3 ones
4 one
5 ours
6 yours

Exercise 6

1 That umbrella is mine.
2 Is that pen yours?
3 He's a friend of mine.
4 She's a colleague of Amy's.
5 Is he a friend of yours?
6 Is that mine or yours? *or* Is that yours or mine?

6 Possessive 's and s'

Exercise 1

1 b
2 a
3 d
4 e
5 c
6 f

Exercise 2

1 teeth	**4** half
2 wives	**5** were
3 feet	**6** are

Exercise 3

1 Keith's
2 My parents'
3 end of
4 week's

Exercise 4

1 What's Alex's dog's name?
2 I've put your coat at the bottom of the stairs.
3 Wayne is starting a new job in a week's time.
4 What are the students' nationalities?
5 What's the name of the hotel where you stayed?
6 You can watch the world's top sportsmen and women at the Olympic Games.

Exercise 5

1 six months' time
2 of the sofa
3 of the swimming pool
4 My wife's
5 the back of
6 London's

Exercise 6

1 father's
2 of the car
3 students'
4 parents'
5 of the tickets

7 Articles and other words before nouns

Exercise 1

1 the	**4** ᵃthe, ᵇa
2 ᵃa, ᵇThe	**5** a
3 a	**6** the

Exercise 2

1 work	**4** bed
2 the dentist's	**5** the theatre
3 hospital	**6** the post office

Exercise 3

1 school yet?
2 the cinema.
3 university in the United States.
4 the airport.
5 the theatre.

Exercise 4

1 My brother ate all my food.
2 I'd like both those dresses.
3 I see my parents every weekend.
4 The boys went to Josh's house every day.
5 The chef broke all the eggs.
6 My other sister is at home.

Exercise 5

1 another	**4** another
2 other	**5** other
3 another	**6** both

Exercise 6

1 any	**4** every
2 some	**5** no
3 other	**6** another

8 Past continuous

Exercise 1

1 travelling	**4** waiting
2 saw	**5** had
3 happened	**6** getting

Exercise 2

1 were you talking to
2 found
3 heard
4 listened
5 saying
6 were you doing

Exercise 3

1 visiting
2 working
3 getting
4 having
5 met
6 dropped

Exercise 4

1 e
2 d
3 f
4 b
5 a
6 c

Exercise 5

1 Yes
2 No
3 No
4 Yes
5 No
6 Yes

Exercise 6

1 was coming
2 saw
3 was cycling
4 dropped
5 was waiting
6 sat

9 There and It sentences

Exercise 1

1 wasn't
2 will
3 Have
4 were
5 Did

Exercise 2

1 Is there a doctor in this building?
2 It has been a wonderful holiday.
3 It won't be easy to find the house.
4 There weren't any problems with the car.
5 Was it cold outdoors last night?
6 There is going to be a storm.

Exercise 3

1 It's
2 It was
3 There's been
4 there have been
5 There was
6 It isn't

Exercise 4

1 Yes
2 No
3 Yes
4 Yes
5 No

Exercise 5

1 Yes
2 No
3 Yes
4 No
5 No
6 No

Exercise 6

1 Is it raining
2 Are there
3 Will it be
4 There was
5 Wasn't there
6 it is going to be *or* it's going to be

10 Questions

Exercise 1

1 are these
2 the next train leaves
3 the door is locked
4 do you open
5 is your sister
6 is her new boyfriend

Exercise 2

1 Which books do you need to take with you?
2 How often do you go to the gym?
3 Can you tell me when the show starts?
4 He asked me where I work.
5 How long is the movie?
6 Why was the letter written in French?

Exercise 3

1 What
2 Which
3 How
4 long
5 How
6 why

Exercise 4

1 b
2 d
3 e
4 a
5 c
6 f

Exercise 5

1 long
2 whose
3 who
4 why
5 like
6 Which

Exercise 6

1 When was the food cooked?

2 How high is the wall?

3 How often are these computers checked?

4 Which pictures do you like best?

5 Can you tell me how to use this machine?

6 Whose story was read to the class?

11 Adjectives

Exercise 1

1 tallest	4 most expensive
2 smarter	5 heavy
3 hotter	

Exercise 2

1 hardest	4 expensive
2 colder	5 difficult
3 smaller	6 better

Exercise 3

1 b	4 d
2 c	5 a
3 e	6 f

Exercise 4

1 busy	4 frightened
2 keen	5 delicious
3 careful	

Exercise 5

1 Yes	4 No
2 Yes	5 No
3 No	6 Yes

Exercise 6

1 What is the best time to visit you?

2 I'm excited about my new car.

3 Nick is younger than everyone in his class.

4 This chair is the least comfortable.

5 Jo is very fond of milk chocolate.

6 Peaches are the sweetest fruit.

12 Link words

Exercise 1

1 or	4 so
2 nor	5 both
3 but	6 that

Exercise 2

1 both	4 nor
2 not only	5 or
3 so	6 and

Exercise 3

1 Yes	4 Yes
2 No	5 No
3 No	6 Yes

Exercise 4

1 or	4 so
2 and	5 but
3 neither	6 nor

Exercise 5

1 His behaviour was neither clever nor funny.

2 The food was not only healthy but also delicious.

3 I was so tired I had to go to bed.

4 Both the car and the bike were stolen.

5 I need either a knife or some scissors.

6 The weather was so bad we decided to go home.

Exercise 6

1 a	4 b
2 e	5 f
3 d	6 c

13 Time clauses

Exercise 1

1 e	4 a
2 f	5 c
3 b	6 d

Exercise 2

1 to	4 although
2 while	5 to
3 when	

Exercise 3

1 although it rained a lot.
2 if you want to watch the news?
3 although it was Saturday.
4 after you had dinner?
5 while you were out.

Exercise 4

1 when   4 before
2 to   5 If
3 although   6 to

Exercise 5

1 Marion can sing while Jeffrey plays the piano.
2 Please make some tea after you've washed the cups.
3 Call this number if you want to make an appointment.
4 Angela texted her parents to give them the good news.
5 Simona didn't take her gloves although it was snowing.
6 Will you buy me a car when you're rich?

Exercise 6

1 Billy, what did you do with the dictionary after you used it?
2 Although I didn't like James, I helped him with his homework.
3 If there is a fire, ring 999.
4 What will you do if I give you all this money?
5 When I am old, I will stay in expensive hotels.
6 Jeremy sent this card to wish me happy birthday.
7 Before you can watch football on television you have to tidy your room.

Exercise 7

1 while   3 if
2 after he has   4 to

14 Zero and first conditionals

Exercise 1

1 e   4 f
2 c   5 b
3 a   6 d

Exercise 2

1 need   4 cook
2 don't work   5 won't have
3 will buy   6 will want

Exercise 3

1 Yes   4 Yes
2 No   5 No
3 No   6 Yes

Exercise 4

1 gives ✓   4 offers ✓
2 he'll make ✗   5 be ✗
3 cooks ✓   6 meet ✗

Exercise 5

1 will be   4 gets
2 invites   5 fail
3 don't eat   6 I'll be

Exercise 6

1 Your jacket will get wet if you leave it outside.
2 If you don't work, you don't earn money.
3 You'll get too hot if you sit in the sun.
4 If I see Julia I'll talk to her.
5 Will you sing if I play the guitar?
6 Will you come to the beach tomorrow if it's sunny?

15 Adverbs

Exercise 1

1 b   4 a
2 c   5 f
3 e   6 d

Exercise 2

1 basically   4 in fact
2 these days   5 down the road
3 practically   6 kindly

Exercise 3

1 in   4 around
2 over   5 here
3 next   6 along

Exercise 4

1 a	**4** c
2 f	**5** b
3 e	**6** d

Exercise 5

1 afterwards	**4** normally
2 finally	**5** occasionally
3 at once	**6** soon

Exercise 6

1 suddenly	**4** luckily
2 in town	**5** afterwards
3 all the way	**6** along the river

16 Adverb position

Exercise 1

1 always goes
2 usually plays
3 see you tomorrow
4 sometimes go
5 never forgets
6 often have

Exercise 2

1 f	**4** d
2 a	**5** b
3 c	**6** e

Exercise 3

1 Yes	**4** No
2 No	**5** Yes
3 No	**6** Yes

Exercise 4

1 Yesterday our family moved
2 a great view over the city
3 see the beach clearly
4 will never
5 Today I put
6 always like

Exercise 5

1 I left my shoes near the door.
2 Can you drive me to the station tomorrow?
3 Make sure you cross the road very carefully.
4 She keeps the cookies on the top shelf.
5 Boris always eats his food very slowly.
6 Did you speak to Beth unkindly yesterday?

Exercise 6

1 yesterday	**4** never
2 badly	**5** afterwards
3 always	**6** politely

17 Modal verbs (1)

Exercise 1

1 Yes	**4** No
2 Yes	**5** No
3 No	**6** Yes

Exercise 2

1 have to	**4** mustn't
2 must not	**5** have
3 don't have	**6** have to

Exercise 3

1 have to	**4** must not
2 can	**5** have to
3 must	**6** able to

Exercise 4

1 No	**4** No
2 Yes	**5** Yes
3 Yes	**6** No

Exercise 5

1 must ✗	**4** were not able ✓
2 could ✓	**5** must ✗
3 don't have to ✓	**6** couldn't ✗

Exercise 6

1 mustn't ✓	**4** not able ✓
2 must ✓	**5** haven't ✗
3 aren't ✗	**6** can ✓

18 Modal verbs (2)

Exercise 1

1 f | 4 c
2 d | 5 e
3 b | 6 a

Exercise 2

1 may come | 4 could call
2 could walk | 5 will probably be
3 might help | 6 might not be

Exercise 3

1 rain | 4 be able
2 run | 5 arrive
3 want | 6 go

Exercise 4

1 No | 4 No
2 Yes | 5 No
3 Yes | 6 Yes

Exercise 5

1 Our team probably won't win the competition.
2 Could you afford to buy a new computer?
3 My parents might give me a laptop.
4 The water may be too cold for swimming.
5 I'll probably ask my mum to come with me.
6 I'm sure that Alfie couldn't see us.

Exercise 6

1 to give ✗ | 4 don't ✗
2 asked ✗ | 5 might ✓
3 stay ✓ | 6 being ✗

19 Modal verbs (3)

Exercise 1

1 No | 4 No
2 Yes | 5 Yes
3 Yes | 6 No

Exercise 2

1 ought not | 4 Ought we
2 should | 5 better
3 better not | 6 Should

Exercise 3

1 to ✗ | 4 Ought ✓
2 oughtn't ✓ | 5 shouldn't ✓
3 should ✗ | 6 better ✗

Exercise 4

1 shouldn't go | 4 ought to ask
2 ought to wear | 5 shouldn't do
3 should rest | 6 'd better not try

Exercise 5

1 better | 4 to
2 not | 5 had
3 not | 6 Ought

Exercise 6

1 ought | 4 ought
2 shouldn't | 5 better not
3 should | 6 better

20 Modal verbs (4)

Exercise 1

1 won't | 5 come
2 Would | 6 Shall
3 'll help | 7 make
4 Will

Exercise 2

1 won't | 4 won't
2 Will | 5 will
3 will | 6 Shall

Exercise 3

1 e | 4 b
2 d | 5 c
3 a | 6 f

Exercise 4

1 Shall I cook the dinner for everyone tonight?
2 My brother won't tell me why he is laughing.
3 Do you think Dad will take me to the airport?
4 Ben says he will write to Emma every day.
5 This jar's lid won't come off.
6 He'll do most of the hard work for you.

Exercise 5

1 Yes	4 Yes
2 Yes	5 No
3 No	6 No

Exercise 6

1 won't ✓
2 will ✓
3 Shall ✓
4 won't ✗
5 shall ✗
6 won't ✓

21 Passive

Exercise 1

1 a	4 c
2 f	5 e
3 b	6 d

Exercise 2

1 given	4 made
2 taken	5 told
3 eaten	6 done

Exercise 3

1 was	4 Were
2 were	5 was
3 was	6 weren't

Exercise 4

1 Have	4 been
2 haven't	5 served
3 Has	6 hasn't

Exercise 5

1 were	4 Have
2 are	5 is
3 has	6 was

Exercise 6

1 given	5 have
2 been	6 cleaned
3 stolen	
4 kept	

22 Question tags

Exercise 1

1 don't you
2 has it
3 are there
4 didn't he
5 haven't they
6 weren't you

Exercise 2

1 c	4 e
2 f	5 d
3 a	6 b

Exercise 3

1 isn't it
2 haven't you
3 haven't they
4 do you
5 isn't she
6 does it

Exercise 4

1 do they ✓
2 wasn't it ✓
3 don't they ✓
4 didn't they ✓
5 aren't they ✗
6 is it ✗

Exercise 5

1 Yes, there are.
2 No, he hasn't.
3 Yes, it was.
4 No, it hasn't.
5 Yes, I have.
6 Yes, there were.

23 Verbs not normally used in continuous forms

Exercise 1

1 d	4 f
2 e	5 c
3 a	6 b

Exercise 2

1	Yes	**4**	Yes
2	No	**5**	Yes
3	No	**6**	No

Exercise 3

1	are feeling	**4**	smell
2	know	**5**	think
3	are thinking	**6**	belong

Exercise 4

1 are seeming ✗
2 are you tasting ✓
3 feels ✓
4 weren't thinking ✓
5 Are you hearing ✗
6 don't seem ✓

Exercise 5

1 You're liking ✗
2 are ✓
3 is having ✗
4 looks ✓
5 I'm thinking ✓
6 you're understanding ✗

Exercise 6

1 's tasting *or* is tasting
2 don't understand *or* do not understand
3 isn't thinking *or* is not thinking
4 knows
5 doesn't like *or* does not
6 don't believe *or* do not believe

24 Verbs followed by two objects

Exercise 1

1 Don't let me forget to buy some stamps at the post office.
2 Stephanie would like you to play tennis with her this afternoon.
3 Do you think you can make the printer start working again?
4 Shall we give Helen a bunch of flowers?
5 Danny wants his friends to visit him while he's in hospital.
6 The visitors took Tom a box of chocolates.

Exercise 2

1	Yes	**4**	No
2	No	**5**	No
3	Yes		

Exercise 3

1	give	**4**	would like
2	helped	**5**	expects
3	taught		

Exercise 4

1	do	**4**	eat
2	to do	**5**	him to be
3	to eat	**6**	him

Exercise 5

1 came ✗
2 cook ✓
3 to know ✗
4 to him ✗
5 to end ✓
6 to have ✓

Exercise 6

1	Yes	**4**	No
2	No	**5**	No
3	Yes	**6**	Yes

25 Pronouns and adjectives

Exercise 1

1	c	**4**	a
2	f	**5**	b
3	e	**6**	d

Exercise 2

1	another coffee?	**4**	other ones?
2	any others?	**5**	another.
3	another one.		

Exercise 3

1	other	**4**	other
2	another	**5**	another
3	others	**6**	another

Exercise 4

1 Does she have any other friends?
2 Would you like another drink?
3 We had a few other problems.
4 Are there any other cakes?
5 Shall we try another café?
6 Could you tell the others?

Exercise 5

1 other	4 another
2 any	5 one
3 the	6 others

Exercise 6

1 others	4 any
2 another	5 one
3 other	6 ones

26 Relative pronouns and reflexive pronouns

Exercise 1

1 Yes	4 Yes
2 Yes	5 Yes
3 No	6 No

Exercise 2

1 other	4 himself
2 yourselves	5 ourselves
3 another	6 each

Exercise 3

1 c	4 f
2 a	5 d
3 e	6 b

Exercise 4

1 yourself	4 ourselves
2 themselves	5 yourselves
3 herself	6 itself

Exercise 5

1 No	4 No
2 Yes	5 Yes
3 Yes	

Exercise 6

1 each	3 myself
2 ourselves	4 who

Exercise 7

1 yourself	4 you
2 which	5 myself
3 each	6 who

27 Phrasal verbs

Exercise 1

1 a	4 f
2 e	5 d
3 c	6 b

Exercise 2

1 b	4 d
2 c	5 e
3 a	6 f

Exercise 3

1 on.	4 switch it off.
2 made it up.	5 got out of his car.
3 found out.	6 put it off.

Exercise 4

1 I switched off the light.
2 Gemma puts her clothes away in the cupboard.
3 Harry made up a story for his children.
4 John found out some information on the Internet.
5 Jill put her coat on in the hall.
6 My sister is looking after my two children.

Exercise 5

1 after	4 out
2 in	5 up
3 off	6 away

Exercise 6

1 up	4 on
2 on	5 for
3 up	6 off

28 Requests, offers and invitations

Exercise 1

1	f	**4**	b
2	c	**5**	e
3	d	**6**	a

Exercise 2

1	look	**4**	to go
2	get	**5**	seeing
3	download		

Exercise 3

1 Not at all, any time. What about pizza for lunch?
2 Would you mind giving me that file? Let's join the tennis club.
3 May I have another cake? Could you tell me the right answer, please?
4 I'm sorry, I'm busy. Let's not do that.

Exercise 4

1 I've just sat down – maybe the next one!
2 Great. I can wear my new walking boots.
3 No, thanks. I'm not hungry.
4 Sure. Here you are.
5 Not at all.
6 Thanks, but I'm busy on Saturday.
7 Of course – but don't break it!
8 I'm sorry, I'm going out with Jim tonight.

Exercise 5

1 Can I help you with your project?
2 Do you need a towel for the beach?
3 Let me do the washing-up.
4 What about a glass of orange?
5 Would you like to come swimming this afternoon?
6 Would you mind helping me with my homework?

Exercise 6

1	No	**4**	Yes
2	No	**5**	No
3	Yes	**6**	Yes

Exercise 7

1 Shall I shut the computer down?
2 What about renting a car on holiday?
3 Can I do anything to help?
4 Do you need anything from the supermarket?
5 Would you like some more pasta?
6 Can you please close the door?

29 Agreeing, disagreeing and telling people what you want and need

Exercise 1

1	Yes	**4**	Yes
2	No	**5**	No
3	Yes		

Exercise 2

1	f	**4**	d
2	e	**5**	c
3	a	**6**	b

Exercise 3

1	must	**4**	needs to
2	needs	**5**	must
3	must		

Exercise 4

1	No	**4**	No
2	Yes	**5**	Yes
3	Yes	**6**	No

Exercise 5

1	agree	**4**	need
2	opinion	**5**	must
3	have	**6**	true

Exercise 6

1 I agree that this computer game is too easy!
2 In my opinion the pictures are quite boring.
3 But it's true that the music's good.
4 I need to get some new games.
5 I'll have to borrow some from my friends.
6 I need to phone them soon.

30 Suggesting, advising and saying that you're sure

Exercise 1

1 d   4 f
2 b   5 a
3 c   6 e

Exercise 2

1 I'm not sure   4 Let's
2 Shall we   5 must
3 You should

Exercise 3

1 Why don't we   4 can't be
2 I'm not sure   5 What about
3 She should

Exercise 4

1 I'm sure
2 could be
3 can't be
4 Let's
5 I think you should
6 I'm sure

Exercise 5

1 No   4 Yes
2 Yes   5 Yes
3 No

Exercise 6

1 be ✓
2 we ✗
3 to ✗
4 have ✗
5 not ✓
6 could ✓

Exercise 7

1 No   4 No
2 Yes   5 No
3 Yes   6 Yes